The Karma Sutra

Sex, Love, and Relationship Zen

By Shelly Wu

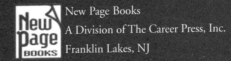

New Page Books
A Division of The Career Press, Inc.
Franklin Lakes, NJ

The Karma Sutra

Edited by Kirsten Dalley

Typeset by Gina Talucci

Cover design by Digi Dog Design/NYC

Printed in the U.S.A. by Book-mart Press

To order this title, please call toll-free 1-800-CAREER-1 (NJ and Canada: 201-848-0310) to order using VISA or MasterCard, or for further information on books from Career Press.

The Career Press, Inc., 3 Tice Road, PO Box 687,
Franklin Lakes, NJ 07417

www.careerpress.com
www.newpagebooks.com

Library of Congress Cataloging-in-Publication Data

Wu, Shelly, 1959-

The karma sutra : sex, love, and relationship zen / by Shelly Wu.

p. cm.

Includes index.

ISBN 978-1-60163-009-4

1. Man-Woman Relationships. 2. Sex instruction. I. Title

HQ801.W9 2008

306.7--dc22

2008006281

Dedication

To all women, past and present, who have bumbled and stumbled, wondered and blundered through the battlefields of love.

Acknowledgments

A special thanks to Barent, Ray, and Tyler, and the entire new generation of young men determined to give the male species an honorable name. And to my own beloved—time was always on our side.

Contents

Part II
Artha: Happiness, Success, and Prosperity

Part III
Kama: Erotic and Sexual Pleasures

Preface

Sex and spirituality may seem odd bed-fellows, but to the ancient Hindus, sex, love, and relationships were divine acts worthy to be studied and perfected.

The universe makes no moral judg-ments; societies do. Views of what is right and what is wrong can change dramati-cally from time to time and from place to place. What is socially acceptable or even encouraged by some cultures may be thought repulsive and abhorrent by others. The universe makes no such distinctions or categories in the reality of what is (that is, the natural consequences of thoughts, intentions, and actions). To pass from delusion to enlightenment means to leave one's fears, judgments, and biases behind.

Western views of the mind were reborn in 1929 when renowned psychologist Carl G. Jung bridged the philosophical gap between East and West with his theory of synchronicity, or meaningful coincidences. In the past few decades, the realization of the unity of spirit, mind, and body finds many in the East and West following similar paths. Self-esteem and self-concept are critical in shaping our attitudes about relationships and sexuality. Our sexual desire begins long before we reach the bedroom. Readying the mind for good relationships is about directing and focusing our energies.

In contrast with certain other religious doctrines, which teach that human nature is something bad and needs to be controlled and sublimated, Eastern concepts of humanity teach that the body is the very residence of the Creator—a testament to his existence and the essence of love. This belief fosters an attitude of joy, a sense of living in the present, and healthy self-esteem. In particular, the Kama Sutra of Vatsyayana teaches how to enjoy and embrace all of the pleasures this life has to offer. It is not a philosophy of self-denial and suffering, but rather one of self-love, self-elevation, enjoyment, and appreciation.

Certain Eastern traditions teach that self-control and enlightenment can be achieved through techniques such as controlled breathing, meditation, and special sexual practices. Both tantric and Taoist concepts of sexuality stress the importance of the frame of mind when engaging in physical love. The following parable illustrates some of the salient concepts presented in this book—namely, that the control of the conscious mind, the influence of intent, and the power of our perceptions can shape our most intimate relationships.

An old Master was teaching his students. He said: "A battle is raging inside of me. It is a fearsome fight between two Tigers. One Tiger represents my fear, anger, envy, selfishness, regret, arrogance, self-pity, shame, resentment, false pride, superiority, and ego. The other Tiger is my love, joy, peace, graciousness, humility, kindness, forgiveness, friendship, empathy, generosity, compassion, and faith."

He continued, "The same battle is raging inside each one of you."

The students thought about this for a while, until one of the students asked his Master, "Which Tiger will win?"

The old Master replied, "The one you feed."

It is my hope that this book will encourage you to always "feed" love and challenge your fears.

Introduction

My second favorite activity is dating—the first is losing consciousness while bungee jumping and smashing face first into a craggy cliff.

Don't get me wrong. I love to be in love. The only problem is that I'm a nut magnet. Really, I am. For years, every weirdo, commitment-phobe, and "perfect storm" of male stupidity found me absolutely irresistible or just had to have me.

Then one day, chilling thoughts of spending another evening listening to some narcissist drone on about his latest act of brilliance, or trying to remove every trace of cat hair from my house to keep the allergic boyfriend from going into anaphylactic shock again, made me swear off all alarming, disordered, neurotic, and overall frightening men (that is, pretty much anyone with a Buzz Lightyear action figure collection or a restraining order). I plunged into monk mode, withdrew from social activities, and refused to answer my e-mails. I meditated, soul-searched, and waited for some kind of an epiphany. I was terrified of becoming the prophet of doom—or worse, my grandmother after her third Manhattan cocktail. So I withdrew, iced my bruised ego, and hid the fact that I was as needy as my mother before starting hormone replacement.

And then, like the proverbial butterfly emerging from its chrysalis, I came out of my shell. My plan was to assemble the "triumvirate of estrogen"—a certain black silk dress that gave me outstanding cleavage; long, shiny locks; and mega-mascaraed lashes that rivaled those of Cleopatra. Meanwhile, as I mentally mapped out the logistics of my Herculean comeback, it happened. *He* happened. Turbo Testosterone Tommy. The urban Adonis of the laundry room. We talked for almost an hour while I oh-so-eagerly answered his every question about detergent measurements. After the hour was up, he confirmed the strong attraction between us by asking me out to dinner in an hour. Suddenly, a terrible thought snapped me out of la-la land: Here was the nicest, hottest, most normal guy I had met in eons and I had less than 60 minutes to pull off the kind of deferred personal maintenance feat attempted only by extreme makeovers or the truly insane. As if that weren't enough, I hadn't shaved my legs for so long that donning a pair of shorts could have easily caused any neighbor to call animal control. In addition, the angry "undergrounder" plowing its way up through my left eyebrow was threatening to make its presence known by nightfall. I had not gotten around to buying that sexy black dress, either (that was on the list after leg defuzzing), or the mega-lash mascara. The best thing I had to wear belonged at the Cairo museum in an airtight vault.

And then, something else hit me. Here I was right back on the same old external relationship track, twisting myself into a pretzel and starving, shaving, plucking, and stuffing myself into the latest packaging—all in hopes of making that connection with Mr. Right. Trying to survive in the singles world had made me as crazy as a pigeon lady—without the birds! I'm a fairly low-maintenance woman, and my needs are minimal. But I'd rather be strapped to a mast and forced to watch a weekend marathon of male erectile enhancement commercials than invest myself in another dead-end relationship. So I got calm, centered myself, and decided to get back to basics—my basics. Karma.

We'll get back to Tommy later. But first, let me explain what I mean by karma and how it influences our relationships.

Author Note

The personal stories throughout the book are compilations and condensations of communiqués I have received through the years from clients requesting relationship advice. All names and identifying details have been changed to protect privacy.

Part I
Dharma:
Spirit, Virtue,
and Ethics

Karma and Your Love Life

1

Love is born from practice.

—Vatsyayana

*J*ust in case you haven't noticed, the universal law of cause and effect is alive and well. Going to sleep tonight isn't going to make your threat to perform a do-it-your-self vasectomy on your boyfriend go away. When you wake up, you will still have to face the consequences of your not-so-veiled threat. Sure he was flirting with your room-mate, but you can expect him to be a little leery of getting near you in a pair of shorts for a while. Karma works in a similar way. Its essence is absolute natural consequences.

In 1687 Sir Isaac Newton recognized a universal truth, a little something he liked to call the laws of motion, and he used these laws to explain the many effects that motion had on physical objects. Newton also taught us that for every force or action, there is an equal and opposite reaction. What Newton couldn't see, prove, or quantify is this same principle in action on the spiritual plane. The spiritual equivalent of natural consequences (or "cause and effect") is what religious philosophers call the law of reaping and sowing. You may have heard the modern version, "What goes around, comes around." There is a law of balance operating in the universe that demands equality. For every win there must be a loss; for every happiness, a sadness; and for every positive move, a negative challenge. You cannot have one without the other; it would be like trying to separate day from night or man from woman. To understand the natural laws of the universe is to also understand the spiritual laws. As the laws of motion form the basis for all physical mechanics, so do certain laws of love form the basis for all "spiritual mechanics." *Whether it be the physical realm or the spiritual realm, cause cannot be separated from effect.*

And that's where we begin.

Karma is Sanskrit for "action" or "deed" in denoting the cycle of cause and effect. It is the sum of all that you have done, are currently doing, and will do in the future. The results, or "fruits," of these actions are called *karma-phala*. Karma is not about retribution, vengeance, punishment, or reward; karma simply deals with what is. From the immediate effects of our *kriyamana* (daily, or "instant") karma—for example, getting caught in a lie or cheating—to the long-term, accumulated debts of *prarabdha* (the future effects of present actions and intentions) karma, each moment of every day we are tipping or balancing the karmic scales.

Any thought, action, or emotion, whether positive or negative, is a pebble cast out onto the serene surface of our relationship ponds. This pebble sends ripples through the water; the larger the pebble, the greater the impact on the pond. This creates changes in the pond as well as in objects on or around the water. We each toss our pebbles (energy) into the universal pond (the collective consciousness—our shared beliefs and attitudes) moment by moment. Learning to accept responsibility for the results (natural consequences) of those tosses, skims, and skips is a lifelong process. But it is imperative that we allow ourselves to learn from, and be shaped by, these consequences.

Although all aspects of our lives are influenced by karma, this influence is most evident in our love lives. The interaction between karma and romance starts even before we are born with our selection of physical attributes, the particular spiritual lessons we must master, and the environments that shape and mold our personalities. Although each love relationship will have its own unique "script," or destiny, what is common to all of them is the potential for growth—the kind of cataclysmic spiritual evolution that unites the ego with the soul.

We immediately evaluate each potential love interest on many levels. Some evaluations are conscious (I love his hair and eyes); some, subconscious (he reminds me of my father); some, personality based (we have so much in common); and some, spiritually based (we recognize each other and have unfinished business from the past). Occasionally, relationships crash and burn because of past karma, rather than due to simple incompatibility. Despite the passionate feelings involved, sometimes we just have to part ways with a beloved person. These kinds of relationships involve a lot of trial and error, and the learning process can feel like birth pains. A difference in spiritual maturity between two partners is responsible for the relationship drama, obsessions, and depressions that you yourself may have survived. In addition to some sleepless nights, these journeys will also create some entertaining (and some not-so-amusing) memories for the rocking chair. But the end result is that both partners learn lessons. Both have completed the purpose for the union.

When walking the tightrope of love and attachment there are only meaningful coincidences. When you first encounter someone, your eyes meet and you see his hair color, eyes, and smile, but you also "see," or sense, his spirit energy (essence). Physical appearance, professional aspirations, or social circumstances can't explain the intense attraction that exists between certain people. This attraction is not based on sexual chemistry alone; rather, it is a "spiritual rendezvous" between kindred and familiar spirits. Sometimes, however, our personalities are so oblivious to the purpose of certain karmic situations that we feel like victims and captives in our own arenas. Not only can relationship karma be a proverbial bitch, but it can also come with no conscious warning. As much as we think we are planning and directing things, relationship karma can charge in like a bull or quietly stalk us like a cheetah.

We are spiritual creatures inhabiting physical bodies. The soul or spirit is the point of consciousness or essence that survives from one life to the next. When our personalities have served their purpose, our souls will quite naturally discard them. Our quest is to bring our personalities into harmony with our destinies, as chosen by our souls. As our choices actively create past, present, and future experiences, we alone are responsible for our lives, and the pain or joy they bring to others.

Could Your Past Be Ruling Your Present?

2

We rarely encounter someone of importance in our lives who doesn't have some foundation in our past. When you start to examine what has been happening in your relationships you may begin to see some patterns. Relationship dynamics are destined to be repeated until they are finally healed or made right. Lovers resolving karma are two souls who meet up once again to learn, resolve issues, reverse roles, and/or generally work out past issues in a new arena. These types of relationships can be identified by the tumult they bring—think of the couples who survive 50 brawling years of marriage. These particular connections are often of the love/hate variety, in which the balance of power is always in question. On again/off again partners and those who divorce and remarry each other find themselves in this pattern, as well.

Never is the concept of "like attracting like" more evident than in the realm of relationships. Opposites may attract on a personality level, but this is never the case on the spiritual level. Those with similar intents gravitate toward one another. Likewise, couples who are fascinated by and initially attracted to each others' personalities or physical appearances, but are dissimilar spiritually, will eventually repel each other due to clashes between bodiless forces. If you've ever wondered why you couldn't seem to disconnect from a distressing love affair, or why you were attracted to someone utterly unsuited to you, relationship karma may be the culprit.

Some nasty karma exists between certain individuals. You might have had the unfortunate experience of being trapped on a road trip with one of these unpleasant pairs. Locked in combat with one another over a myriad of unseen issues, these couples can make the Fourth of July seem tranquil. Amongst these couplings are found previous enemies, rivals, and antagonists. The jailed meets his or her jailer and the duped meets his or her trickster, but this time each is wiser and experienced enough to do some real reciprocal damage. These are the worst of the worst karmic love combinations and the stuff of which the domestic disturbance police call is made. On a brighter note, the same dynamic responsible for antagonistic pairings also produces torrid love affairs, love triangles, and memorable love scenes. From soul mates and twin flames to obsessions and fatal attractions, interlocked destiny happens!

Fresh insights, new arenas, and different choices are offered to us as we search for inspiration, learn from our mistakes, and perfect our spiritual character. Fate will assist us and steer that familiar soul into our path, but our destiny will ultimately be determined by what we choose to do with our opportunities, as well as the natural consequences of our choices.

Soul Partnerships

3

Joy ('joi), n. The passion or emotion excited by the acquisition or possession of what we love or desire.

Happiness ('ha-p´-nə^s), n. An agreeable feeling arising from good fortune of any kind.

(Source: The Collaborative International Dictionary of English)

Affairs of the heart preoccupy most of us. They bring the highest highs and the lowest lows. Enticement, affection, and love all originate at a soul level. Significant people come into our lives at appointed times. We are presented with many choices throughout our lives, and many people who will, each in his or her own way, take us down a certain life path. Because we are spiritual creatures contained within physical shells, the ultimate purpose of our earthly existence is not physical development, but, rather, spiritual or soul development. Each potential partner carries his or her own unique combination of spirit-improving or spirit-destroying potentials.

It has been said that there is a special someone for all of us. Actually, there are many special someones with whom we could be very happy. By being in synch with the universal laws of spiritual motion we can attract those partners who will further our spiritual, mental, and physical happiness. We need not look far to find significant connections in our lives. Although it is sometimes true that opposites attract each other, in the spiritual realm, like attracts like. Kindred or familiar souls gravitate toward each other and seek to reunite once again. The safety of sameness brings like-minded couples together because they know that their intents will be held in common.

It is sometimes difficult to differentiate between infatuation, lust, and love. As a spiritual connection is the first and most basic support for a successful relationship, one must ask the critical questions: Will a certain romantic alliance make me a better person? Is this a balanced relationship of give and take, or does this attachment contribute only discouragement, continually bringing out the worst in me? One's potential, one's joy, and one's higher purpose can all be destroyed by uniting with the wrong person.

Spiritual and soul mate relationships are unions in which both people have been brought together to achieve a common goal of some kind. A true soul mate can be identified as one who walks alongside of another in support and agreement of purpose. Soul mates share a life goal and steadfastly work together to achieve it. In addition, each person contributes to the personal growth of the other. However, this doesn't mean that two soul mates won't experience friction; indeed, each may feel that the other person is the source of their pain at times. The soul mate "mirrors" the other and spiritually enables the partner to develop his or her strengths and confront his or her weaknesses. The fact is that we cannot grow spiritually until we have the courage to enter into relationships of spiritual depth.

Karmic connections, or "soul partnerships," are pairings between spiritual equals. Those who consciously choose to act from the spiritual parts of their personalities are naturally drawn to one another. They may be colleagues at work, lovers, fellow students, spouses, in-laws, or even neighbors. The common spiritual awareness is what brings them together. A successful soul partnership requires:

1. Awareness of the spirit part of your "selfhood equation." Soul/spirit (sometimes called temperament) plus personality (emotions, preferences, and character) equal self.

2. Awareness of feelings. Cultivate your ability to identify the source of your feelings (fear based or love based). Emotions are critically instructive, and taking notice of them is a direct window to your spirit. Emotions such as fear, jealousy, resentment, and anger reveal their source as personality based, whereas emotions such as happiness, love, joy, and compassion reveal their source to be from spirit.

3. Awareness and control of thoughts, intents, and actions. Be aware of positive impulses and actions such as helpfulness, empathy, and encouragement, as well as negative impulses and actions such as revenge, ridicule, judging, and comparing yourself to others.

4. Accepting responsibility for those thoughts, intents, and actions. Don't dodge this by blaming, judging, needing to be right, demanding admiration, escaping into thoughts (intellectualizing), or trying to convince. Always let the

spiritual parts of your personality inform and guide your intentions before you act.

5. Awareness of attachment. This can be seen in expectations, manipulations, and deceptions. Cultivate the ability to release your expectations of, or reliance on, certain preconceived outcomes.

6. Awareness of all six senses, including intuition.

7. A successful uniting of spirit and personality.

Soul mates are aware that there is a specific reason for their union. Each one will learn important lessons about him- or herself from interactions with the other. Soul partners are also committed to examining themselves closely and learning from one another. They know that what you want to criticize in your partner usually reveals what you are in need of changing within your own Self. They also know that they are more than bodies and minds, and are together in order to grow spiritually. Obstacles will arise in their relationship, but the difference is that soul partners expect this and work through it. That is what soul partnership means: finding the one who will help you reconcile and ultimately unite the two distinct parts of yourself—your personality and your spirit.

How Will I Know if He Is Mr. Right?

The head, or mind, is a stubborn and rigid taskmaster that deals with facts and logic. It sets expectations, rationalizes, and judges. It is controlling, and a difficult force to contend with in love. This is the part of you that says, "It'll never work," or "All men are the same." It is the head that says, "He's too short," or "My mom would hate him." The heart, or body, on the other hand, is the feeling part of ourselves. This is our soft, vulnerable underbelly that sometimes gets us into trouble. This is the part that is awash in mood-altering hormones, skewing our perceptions and allowing rejection and disappointment to devastate us. This is the part of you that says, "I'll give up everything for this person," or "I want to float on a cloud with him and never come down."

In most relationships, the heart (body) and the head (mind) are not in agreement with each other. Because of this, the soul, or spirit, steps in. The soul intercedes between the rational head and the emotional heart. The soul is our inner voice, our intuition, and our spiritual essence. Two soul mates don't think with their heads or feel with their hearts; they sense their rightness for each other in "soul language." When two soul mates gaze into each other's eyes, they are filled with a charge of energy. They are inspired to do just about anything to take care of the other person. When the two make love, there is a feeling of unity and a shared envelopment of the other. When two soul mates are apart, they don't feel quite right; it's as if something is missing. When they are together, they feel at peace. You get the idea.

Are All Relationships Karmic?

4

A karmic connection is a powerful psychic connection, a spiritual chemistry between two people. It is the successful reuniting of spirit, mind, and body with a matching (also called "kindred" or "familiar") soul that our spirit picks up time and again in various times and places. These relationships can occur between spouses, between parents and children, between best friends, between work colleagues, and even between ourselves and a beloved pet; however, those that occur in a sexual or love relationship context are extraordinarily profound.

Although all relationships have a distinct purpose, there are some that are particularly karmic in nature. These include: obsessive love, sexual addictions, victim/victimizer syndromes, rescued/rescuer scenarios, loyalty/infidelity cycles, and codependent/controller behavior. Unraveling these tangled webs requires learning the lessons that each relationship is destined to teach. This levels the playing field and converts the negative into positive, the fear into courage, and the bitterness into love.

You alone are the sole authority on your spiritual development, and you alone have control over your love destiny. Your spirit knows what it's doing; your job is to get quiet enough to listen. This is the beauty of meditation or prayer— a stilling of the external so that the internal can be heard. Using your intuition and intentions, act from your spirit and challenge the fearful parts of your personality daily.

We each have loving/spiritual parts of ourselves and antagonistic/fearful parts of ourselves. Becoming aware of which part has control—which tiger we feed—is the first step to taking charge. Being aware of your true intent and the motivations behind your actions is the next step. Feelings of unworthiness lead to spirit-less decisions. Spirit-less decisions are those absolutely awful choices we have all made, which run the gamut from the fairly benign (saying something you regret) to the truly traumatic (living with an abusive partner). All of these originate from fear in the personality, and not from the spirit. This is what you want to fix by consciously taking control of your thoughts and intentions, acting only from spirit.

Antagonistic/fearful decisions produce:	Loving/spiritual decisions produce:
Hate	Joy
Fear	Love
Anger	Agreement
Resentment	Forgiveness
Jealousy	Acceptance
Manipulation	Freedom
Bad Intent	Good Intent
Pain	Contentment
Vengeance	Gratitude

Once you do this, others tune into your spiritual "radio station" and you become a magnet for a partner who thinks similarly—a true soul partner who is on the same wavelength with you and who "gets" you. All relationships are really divine alliances and have much larger ramifications than just the here and now. There are no victims, only students. There are no adversaries, only teachers.

Love, Karmic Style:
The Preliminaries

5

> *And they lived happily ever after—*
> *for a while.*
>
> —Shelly Wu

Why do some people live happily ever after while others move from one negative love affair to another? Spiritual dynamics influence why you love or have aversions to certain people. From the perspective of reincarnation and karma, there are only meaningful coincidences. Everything happens for a reason. We experience heart joy or heartbreak because of our karma. Romantic or love karma is the result of our past choices and actions. It is the natural process of cause and effect from both this life and past lives, whether we remember them or not. Someone with good love karma may have acted out of integrity, love, and compassion more often in past relationships. Conversely, someone with bad love karma may have acted out of dishonesty, selfishness, or disloyalty more often in past relationships. Before you feel guilty for any bad love karma, however, it is important to realize that we have *all* been male and female, old and young, strong and weak, quick and slow, kind and brutal.

As we will see in Chapter 8, some of our relationship dramas have their origins in the spiritual realm, as well. These dramas can include emotionally charged subjects such as commitment, intimacy, abandonment, abuse, and obsession, among others. Most of us have bumbled our way through relationships quite sincerely out of ignorance or fear, rather than malice. So before you spend agonizing hours obsessing and trying to deconstruct Mr. Wonderful's intentions, remember: If it looks like a tree, feels like a tree, and smells like a tree, it probably is a tree. *Trust your feelings.* A man will swim the deepest ocean and climb the highest mountain when he is truly interested in a woman. The male brain and psyche are wired to pursue—you. When a man loves a woman, no obstacle, no war, no distance, no *anything* will keep him from the side of the woman he desires.

Women are natural nurturers, and are more prone to second-guessing than are men. We want to try to figure him out, to fix him. We make excuses for the men in our lives and then lament the consequences. He is not a child who "just isn't feeling well" or is "tired and needs his nap." "Stuff happened" and "I have an early start tomorrow" are clearly lame excuses and are *not* acceptable. These and others are major red flags to a savvy woman to abandon this love boat. Short of being strapped into a straightjacket, nailed into a Houdini box, and immersed in 30 feet of water, a man will always find a way to see you. If he has the will, he will find the way. You can see how ridiculous it is to make excuses for him. Frustration should be a foreign concept in any relationship of substance. Whether you are trying to get him to commit, to spend more time with you, or even just to call more frequently, you are experiencing frustration—and men who love their women don't frustrate them.

Mixed Messages Malone has a fear of confrontation. He won't be straight with you because he has a deep-seated fear of being the victim of an upset, raging, screaming woman. This can probably be traced to the early years of his relationship with the first woman in his life, his mother. No man, really, wants to feel like a scolded, naughty little boy. This man can be elusive and send mixed messages, but as he sees it, it just makes life easier. What we women must remember is that what he says counts very little, but what he does is huge. Although the modern male may not be planning a hunting strategy for his nightly dinner anymore, he still likes to pursue and conquer the woman he desires. A man will strategize and pull off some truly amazing feats to secure the woman he desires. The truth is that if he were truly in love with you, wild horses couldn't keep him away. A "Mr. Perfect" who is no closer to a proposal now than he was last year at this time or the year before that, frankly doesn't think you are worth the investment. If he did, he would have signed, sealed, and delivered that deal long ago. This can be a shattering revelation for a long-suffering girlfriend who thinks that if she is just patient enough, he will eventually come around.

Rule Number One: If He Doesn't Want You, You Don't Want Him

Many years ago, my aunt found me weeping backstage before a community play performance. I was 16 years old and reeling from being dumped by my first serious boyfriend. The pain was fresh and felt unbearable. I knew that I was about to come face to face with him on stage in front of the entire community. For a moment, I didn't know if I could do it. My aunt, who was a no-nonsense kind of lady, took my tear-streaked face in her hands, looked into my eyes, and said, "If he doesn't want you, you don't want him." I would not appreciate the implications of these simple yet wise words for many years. I share them with you now as sincerely and directly as she spoke them to me. Always remember, if he doesn't want you, you definitely don't want him!

A savvy single female will only be interested in guys who are interested in her. By "interested," I'm not talking about Testosterone Tommy looking for a booty call. Sex aside, a man who is truly enamored will call you, e-mail you, message you, and want to be with you as much as is humanly possible. He can't help it. There will be no need to try to persuade, prod, or manipulate him for more time, more sex, more of anything. Second-guessing his motives, planning strategies, or postulating that he's been abducted by aliens are all lessons in futility. A man will crawl, limp, or drag himself if necessary to the nearest phone or communication device. He will call, no matter how busy he is, because you are on his mind throughout the day. He won't disappear on the weekends with no explanation, and he won't want to have sex with anyone else, either. So no more selective inattention and ignoring the reality right in front of you. Remember the tree metaphor: Let's make sure yours is a sturdy oak and not a sickly sapling.

Rule Number Two: If He Can Live Without You, You Can Live Without Him

The damage and negative karma created by holding on to a dead-end relationship or being relegated to a pleasant distraction is profound. Having a witty friend with benefits is cool and all, but you're investing spiritual energy in something that isn't going to give much back. If you're interested in something more—and you should be—accept that this man is not for you. He may have intimacy issues, he may be love-avoidant, or he may have been wounded by a childhood that taught him to equate being close with being "consumed." Whatever the reason, you must accept the fact that he is involved in his own spiritual process, which probably doesn't include you.

Are Some Souls Born to Be Together?

Many transcendent and enlightened minds have thought so. The belief that there is someone special for everyone is not a modern concept. Souls tend to group together in "soul family" units, which can be reunited from different generations, eras, and locales. It is not uncommon to have two, three, or even four or more people with whom you will share a special kind of relationship in this life. You are psychically and eternally joined at the hip with them. One person's physical appearance and even their gender may be different, but your spirit still recognizes him or her. We all possess this kind of spiritual discernment, but the trick is to learn about it and practice using it.

This is a good news/bad news situation. The bad news is that the noise, fast pace, and stress of modern existence bombarding our senses makes it very hard to tune into ourselves. The good news is that once you learn how to listen to your intuition, it's not something you will forget; in that sense it's similar to riding a bicycle. Another positive is that the very idea of predestined soul mates has its roots planted deeply in the concept of reincarnation. The cornerstone of reincarnation is that once relationship lessons are learned, we won't need to repeat them. We are perpetual, eternal students in that regard, and will always be paired with someone in need of our awareness and whose destiny is in sync with our own.

No relationship is merely coincidental. We are spiritual creatures—eternal souls—inhabiting physical bodies. We still must face our own unique challenges, but if we are aware and soulfully awake, we will begin to recognize some powerful allies. These allies are other souls provided in the here and now to walk beside us on a sometimes arduous path toward personal enlightenment. Ancient divination practices such as Vedic and Chinese astrology, as well as numerology, have been used for thousands of years to help identify some of these karmic cycles and connections. We are not meant to share every lifetime together. Instead, we come together at certain times to grow and to work out karmic issues. Each relationship provides important lessons toward growth. If we look at partnerships from that perspective, how can we justify holding grudges or being bitter?

From one relationship we may learn that our happiness resides within us alone, and from another we may learn not to see our self-worth through another's eyes. Some relationships teach us to be strong, to fight back, and to defend ourselves. Other partnerships, despite their pain, convince us that we are indeed special, unique, and worthy of love. This is the quest that all women and men, everywhere and through all time, have shared.

Accepting the possibility that love may indeed be pre-destined pretty much forces us to leave behind that comfortable, familiar self-image of being the romantic victim. Instead of feeling tossed about like a flimsy rowboat—always hopeful, always looking for Mr. Right—we can move into an attitude of creative control of our romances. The nonphysical reality of love and partnerships has the potential to reacquaint the human personality with its spirit. Understanding relationship dynamics by perceiving what really lies beneath them makes it possible to orchestrate alliances. Accepting responsibility for being the creator of your romantic reality is a powerful step.

Self-mastery, loving intention, and being tuned into your own internal spiritual frequency are the keys to recognizing meaningful romantic opportunity. Feelings are not as deceptive as some would have you believe. Yes, they can be and are influenced by a powerful biochemical component of hormones; however, feelings are the nerves of the soul. Use these trusted emotions to sense if someone in your life right now is a natural helper and trusted soul for you. Let your feelings rise above past painful experiences and steer you back onto a course of authentic love, karmic style!

The desire for passionate love is much more than a culturally instilled notion of romanticism. To merge with another person—body, mind, and spirit—is a universal drive. When two souls who are destined to be together unite, three things happen: the conscious mind collapses its ego boundaries, the body "marinates" in a potent cocktail of brain hormones, and the two spirits begin to fuse.

Powerful forces are at play when it comes to when, where, and how you will be reunited with your beloved. Sexual attraction and the exquisite feeling of falling in love may help form an initial bond between two people, but the glue that sets the relationship is the spiritual bond between the two souls. Conducting all of our relationships with affection, compassion, and mutual respect opens up unlimited possibilities for deep and meaningful love connections to develop.

Edgar Cayce, known as the "sleeping prophet," believed that certain people are romantically predestined for one another. He described soul mates as "those of any spiritual sect or group where there is answering (accountability) of one to another. Necessary then, becomes the proper 'fit' of those souls who are 'the answers' to one another." He continues by asserting that "certain souls are 'well knit' before birth. As the tongue is to the groove, they compliment and help one another mentally and spiritually." Cayce also noted that "it may be depended upon, that about 20 percent is absolute (divinely destined) and 80 percent will depend upon 'application'—what the mind (freewill) chooses" (Frejer, 288–1556 passim).

I am a firm believer that nothing happens by chance— and certainly not something as significant as a love relationship. In a universe ruled by cause and effect, life is a continuum of choices and their repercussions. Our present love liaisons are only a renewing of former ties, purposes, and ideals, and are a continued outgrowth from spirit. Love is predestined in that we have different and unique karma with each love partner. Some relationships are to assist and some are to test. There is always a reason that two people unite, whether that reason is unfinished business, lessons to be learned, or a project to complete. Never by chance but by choice, love and its expressions are purposeful. The purposes can be difficult to understand, but they exist nevertheless. You have your own unique "love script" that is woven into your relationship karma. During certain periods of your life you may attract partners who will challenge your abandonment issues. Other cycles may be more conducive to monogamous, committed relationships, while still others may involve independence and self-sufficiency.

When, through fate, we meet a soul mate, the choices we make will determine our destiny. As we become aware of ourselves as more than bodies and a set of personality characteristics, we also become aware that all of our partnerships are purposeful and meaningful experiences. Focus shifts from looking at externals to examining the more meaningful realm of a potential partner's inner landscape.

Identifying Spiritual Companions: Soul Mates and Twin Souls

6

Place me like a seal over your heart;
for love is as strong as death, its jealousy
unyielding as the grave.

—Song of Solomon, 8:6

The idea of soul mates has existed from time immemorial, and can conjure up some very strong feelings—both positive and negative—for a reason. These are the most potent of the karmic connections, and are comprised of familiar souls attached spiritually from previous associations. They are drawn together in the present because of their connection in the past. Passionate in the original sense of the word (meaning "to suffer"), neither one may fully recover emotionally if they are separated. Whether we seek a soul mate who will assist us in our spiritual growth or a twin soul who joins with us to complete an important work or fulfill a purpose, love and desire originate at a soul level.

Among these unforgettable connections are the karmic cohorts, the twin flames, and those who are best suited to assist us in our spiritual development. Typically this takes place within a partnership between two people who decide to live and grow together in physically intimate circumstances and share their sexuality. Soul mates can be incarnated with you in the present or can be acting as guides from the other side, encouraging and helping you. Soul mates are those with whom you share a compatibility that is well above the ordinary. It is that certain something, the unseen love chemistry of the ages. The most memorable moments you will ever have will be with your soul mates. (I say "mates" because it is possible to have more than one.) Your soul mates know you intimately and have already shared many intense bonding experiences with you.

You may ask, "How will I know if someone is a soul mate? How can I determine if a relationship has long-term potential or is just a passing fancy?" Some relationships are truly karmic in nature whereas others are simply partnerships of convenience. The spiritual laws of motion will always link you with whomever you match in energy. There is no need to go searching for a soul mate, as connected souls have an ongoing affinity that neither time nor mortality can separate. The "love at first sight" phenomenon, often experienced by soul mates, is a good indication that you are meeting someone you have formerly loved. In addition, soul mates almost always will share a life goal and work together to achieve it. They are spiritually and mentally on the same page. Couples in this divine alliance quite naturally support one another, forgive past mistakes, and allow for human frailty in the relationship.

If you want to have relationships of depth, commit to your own spiritual growth. As you begin to enjoy your own spiritual cultivation you will also attract like-minded lovers as an extra bonus. Furthermore, as you develop into the person you were destined to be, those who do not share your intentions, choices, and spiritual vibrations will simply leave. Whether we recognize them in the moment or in retrospect, these karmic relationships will inevitably unfold before us— we have only to recognize them.

The Beloved

Every human being has a twin soul, or "beloved." Although we may enjoy the support and love of many soul mates throughout our lives, the beloved creates the potential for indescribable harmony and perfect fusion. If you are fearful that someone may "steal" your partner (and nothing can keep this from happening), it is because that partner is not truly your beloved, not your true twin soul. Twin souls recognize each other with absolute certainty and can never truly leave one another.

Where is my twin soul, and how can we reunite?

Your twin soul may actually be very near—possibly someone you have known all your life or someone just on the sidelines of your life, awaiting the last steps you both need to take in growing in order to reunite. The true union can only take place after the point of reunion has occurred within ourselves, and our male (yang) and female (yin) energies are balanced within. When the spirit, body, and mind are ready, the spiritual partner will appear.

Mary, 42, describes it this way:

> *I have known my twin soul from the very young age of 14. I knew then that he was special. Along the way, somehow we parted, yet, he was always in my heart.... Then one day, middle aged, depressed and thinking that true love had eluded me, "He" appeared as if by divine determination, and it was as if we had never been apart. Very unexpectedly, he came back into my life and psychically by my side once again. And when he looks into*

my eyes...there's nothing else that matters.... I know that I am home. I know I am the one whom he should hold through the night.

Never give up on love; it could be just over the horizon waiting for you. Sometimes fairy tales *do* come true!

The Anatomy of
Bad Relationship
Karma

Your destiny is the reason for your present existence, the plan etched on a spiritual plane before you were even born. When we lose our way, fate is that set of dreaded circumstances that turns us back toward our destiny. Destiny involves free will and choice, whereas fate tends to be out of our hands. During our lifetime, many events will seem unfair or even downright cruel. Whether an injury is minor, such as the sting of unjustified criticism, or major, such as the grief sustained from a betrayal, the experience can be far reaching and life altering.

There are certain types of relationship karma that require us to learn some tough lessons. The particular lessons that need to be mastered determine the timing of our relationships. Some common lessons involve the following scenarios: victim and victimizer; betrayal and infidelity; revenge and retribution; rescuers; obsessive or unrequited love; dependency and people pleasing; and promises, pacts, and vows. All of these tend to entail some kind of power struggle or imbalance, which in turn leads to manipulation, rejection, abandonment, and/or betrayal. These are some of the bitterest disappointments and lessons that we can experience.

A difference in spiritual maturity between partners can lead to misunderstandings and estrangement despite the love the two may share. Often, it is only through these hardships that we discover our inner strengths and gain motivation to achieve our dreams. Once the lessons are learned, any negative energy is converted to its opposite positive manifestation. We subconsciously choose every relationship so that we can grow within and develop our spiritual graces of love, kindness, mercy, and service. Many relationships will involve disappointments, personality clashes, and some hard knocks before the necessary spiritual growth can be accomplished. The trick is to identify those partners who will help and not hinder this growth.

Bad Karma—Attracting Negative Relationships

Bad karma is best described as the intent of the human personality in conflict with the intent of the spirit or soul. Good karma is established when we act in the best interest of our whole being—body, mind, and soul—rather than just one part. For example, One-Night-Stand Man (more on him in Chapter 9) satiates only his physical desires, neglecting his other vital parts, which are left out in the cold. Due to past choices that were scripted from fear rather than love, we have all created bad karma or karmic debt—largely owing to our inexperience and lack of multisensory understanding. We each have our turn as both victim and victimizer, helper and hinderer, "dumpee" and "dumper." What our ignorance or selfishness has produced in the past our personalities will experience in the present, and the more spiritually sensitive we are the greater will be our reaction to these experiences. We are offered the chance to offset negative karma by taking control and intervening intentionally, through choice.

The secret to breaking the vicious cycle of failed relationships is to identify and release negative patterns of thinking. If you want to attract a partner who will participate in a spiritual partnership of depth and duration, your "sticky tape" is confidence and self-esteem. Relationships that accept and enhance the confident you will thrive, but the ones that rely on your negative self-image will not. You can remove the barriers to good relationships by "tuning" your own thoughts and intentions to the right "channel." The only guys who will be able to pick up your signals are those on your same frequency. The truth is, we reshape our romances by reshaping ourselves. Upbeat, loving women who are committed to improving their spiritual condition will attract men of similar thinking. The question is, are you really ready to release those negative patterns?

Karmic Lessons

Victim and victimizer

Whether you are the innocent or guilty party in this type of karmic interaction, it is about unresolved control issues. The imbalance of power prohibits either person from growing spiritually and emotionally. Fear, powerlessness, and suffering are the fundamental steps of this dysfunctional relationship dance. This type of relationship karma tends to be solved by the victim when it's time to take back the power he or she has given up in the relationship. This type of rendezvous brings quantum leaps in spiritual development and maturity for both souls, whether victim or victimizer.

Betrayal and infidelity

Attention, companionship, lust, opportunity, and revenge comprise just some of the personality-based motivations for cheating. Whether it's a sexual infidelity or another form of trust violation, betrayal hurts. The needed lessons from these painful scenarios are diverse. They range from understanding the needs of another to forgiveness. Relationships that involve betrayal carry with them some particularly heady karma. A choice is presented, this time in a new time and place, for the betrayed to either abandon the relationship permanently or forgive the person involved. This type of relationship karma can also be complicated by the addition of a third party.

Revenge and retribution

Karma isn't about punishment; it's about learning the lessons of cause and effect. However, some of these lessons can involve revenge and retribution, in which the betrayed or rejected partner is somehow compensated, and the partner who did the betraying or rejecting finds the shoe on the other foot this time around. This type of karmic lesson doesn't carry the "head trips" and sleepless nights that some of the others do. Because of the reparation and balancing aspects, deep emotional scars are surprisingly rare in revenge and retribution scenarios. The lessons are ostensibly about loyalty and accepting rejection, but they are really about balancing the karmic scales, tit for tat.

Rescuers

Technically speaking, a rescuer is someone who frees or delivers another from captivity, danger, or violence. In psychological terms, however, a rescuer is a person who has a penchant for getting involved with troubled partners. Although rescuing another may seem a rather noble, if not innocuous, activity, its roots can be traced deep into the ground of our self-esteem. A codependent person who takes responsibility for fulfilling the needs of another does it to feel worthy. Many times the rescuer's self-image is on some shaky soil. The mistaken belief is that by taking care of others, he or she will be cared for as well. Ironically, those who rescue others from their follies end up feeling insecure and unappreciated, and will eventually run dry emotionally. The karma of the rescuer is the result of excessive duty, burden, and responsibility. The karmic lesson for the rescuer is that the one being rescued must accept responsibility for the results of his or her choices. Our choices and intents shape and create our reality. Rescuing only prolongs the effect because the cause hasn't been addressed. Rescuing behavior in relationships is emotionally exhausting and cannot result in any kind of permanent solution.

Obsessive love

Obsessive or unrequited love is fairly common, and is the stuff of which novels are written. The beloved is the obsessive lover's favorite subject. Friends and family are alienated as they grow weary of all thoughts, comments, and conversations centered on the beloved. The most trivial fact about the beloved is a matter of great import. Trapped in fear and lacking in self-worth, the loving one worships the beloved as she would a god. The excruciating sting of unrequited or unequal love has its roots planted deeply in the self-esteem of the adorer. The desperate pinings of unrequited love are the most heartbreaking to hear.

Obsessive love is an extreme case of power imbalance. The happiness or unhappiness of the afflicted is at the mercy of the idealized lover. The smallest crumb from the beloved can send the adoring one into heights of ecstasy or crashing and burning in despair. Every word or action of the beloved is microanalyzed for hopeful signs of reciprocity. Obsessive love is always about fear and seeking love from outside oneself. Self-love and acceptance are the lessons to be learned, and the keys to releasing these shackles.

Dependency and people pleasing

Helplessness and neediness only attract codependent, dysfunctional relationships. Karmic relationships that involve dependency concern issues of self-love. If you don't acknowledge and love yourself, you cannot attract healthy relationships. Depending on other people for your happiness is a convenient way to hide from your feelings. Dependent women are fearful women, fearful of feeling painful emotions. Dependent people will always find either a rescuer or a controller/victimizer to complete their script. All three have karmic issues with authority to work out. This karmic lesson is about confronting the pain that lies beneath dependent behavior. People pleasers must learn to love themselves.

Promises, pacts, and vows

Promises, pacts, and vows made at other times and places, and the resulting relationship karma, can carry over to the present. This is because pacts made with strong intent create memories, which are then stored in our subconscious. (Accessing this deep, alpha level of memory by way of meditation will be discussed further in Chapter 13.) A promise to everlasting love made with great emotion or conviction can restrict finding love with anyone other than that person. When two souls agree to love only each another, to the exclusion of all others, forever can be a long time. The lesson to be learned here is often a case of "be careful what you wish for." Most oppressive are the pacts that are open-ended, with no set time limit or "expiration date." These can create interferences when the two people find themselves in a relationship outside of the pact. There is frequently a sadness, as if something were missing in that new relationship. Confirmed bachelors, spinsters, and others with commitment issues are frequently experiencing this type of relationship karma. Other not-so-nice pledges and vows can visit revenge upon other people, relentlessly crossing the limits of each lifetime. Usually made with malice or ill will, revenge pacts can carry over to future lives.

Pledges between two or more people concerning religion, war, patriotism, or injustice are responsible for fanaticism, martyrdom, and zealotry in this life. The intensity of something worth fighting and dying for indelibly imprints these pledge legacies in our memories. An example might be couples who meet and thrive within religious cults and other loyalty-based organizations. Sometimes the fates will use people with this karma to righteously repay a wrong or object to a tyrant.

Lessons learned

Past-life karma is constantly being brought into our present lives. Your spiritual Self chooses certain partnerships and connections with the specific purpose of undergoing a learning experience. The purpose of all of these reunions is to develop the inner qualities that foster your spiritual growth, and change the negative patterns that restrain your spiritual growth. These are the patterns you learn from, and your spiritual development, for better or for worse, depends on it. Remember: no matter how your previous relationships ended, you share some responsibility for their failures as well as their successes. The surest way to be unable to move past these relationships is to not acknowledge the causes that produced the effects. If the underlying issues are not challenged, you will leave this life with the same patterns of relationship karma still intact. Making things right involves learning the lessons your soul yearns to teach. Exploration of the roots of these types of karmic relationships takes great courage, but is worth every ounce of effort. When karma has been completed, a feeling of relief and closure occurs. This is your destiny. The day you truly believe this, your love relationships will never be the same.

So let's get down to the nitty-gritty and take your love life back, shall we?

How Sex Affects Your Karma: Fears, Blocks, and One-Night Stands

8

Joe, 34, goes through significant others the way some men go through socks. He describes his love life this way:

> I don't think I'll ever be truly happy with any one woman. They all get to me in time. I don't understand those couples who do everything together. I just don't see how someone can handle being with the same person that much. Working

together, living together, sleeping, eating, breathing and all. I'd freak out and run. I think the only woman I could handle for a long time would have to be rich and beautiful, classy and slutty, trashy and sophisticated, a slave and a master, a good housekeeper and a slob, dependable and surprising. And I could add more, but I'd still probably dump her because she was too complicated!

You may laugh (and wonder who's dating this guy!), but how do we, the nut magnets, get caught up in these dysfunctional relationship dances in the first place? Many of us are drawn into these dead-end alliances because our "love trains" derailed some time ago (probably sometime around puberty). Others *are* drawn to these superficial men because of unfinished business. Whatever the psychological specifics, the underlying reality is that your relationships are being orchestrated by the spiritual state of your karma.

Feelings are informative! When a relationship is challenging your comfort zone there is a reason for that. Be cautious, and never invest more of your heart than you can bear to lose. In order to do this, it is imperative that you tune into, and listen to, your intuition. I like to call this the EWO (eyes-wide-open) principle.

One-Night Stands

Generation X may not call it a one-night stand anymore (preferring terms such as "hook-up" or "booty call"), but the reasons for one-night stands are still the same—namely, to avoid painful feelings and shore up damaged self-esteem. Many of us have been set adrift on the sea of low expectations in a leaky raft of low self-esteem. We settle for these relationships, hoping we can eventually put down anchor and enjoy life in our little love cove. Contemporary romance tends to involve an attraction to certain mutable external qualities, rather than to the actual person (spirit). When these external qualities change (and they inevitably do), a vicious cycle is born as these traits are sought in someone else, and then someone else, and so on and so on. Enter One-Night-Stand Man, or ONSM (the modern descendant of Post-Neolithic Pete and Neanderthal Ned).

At the core of all compulsive sexual behavior (and two or more one-night stands qualify as compulsive, in my opinion) is the desire to avoid intimacy. When we engage in sex that is devoid of any emotional or spiritual component, we are, in fact, avoiding intimacy. Sex without intimacy is exploitive. Avoiding intimacy is really about running away from desperately painful feelings of worthlessness, powerlessness, and alienation. When we engage in sex with another person, and our physical energies are tapped but our emotional or spiritual selves are not, the result is a psychic imbalance that creates a vicious cycle of psychological and physiological dysfunctions—which themselves generate more addictive, pain-numbing attraction.

Sexual intimacy combined with emotional intimacy involves a very different dynamic. Sexual partners are *not* interchangeable in loving and intimate relationships. We cannot have a sexual encounter with another person without also establishing an emotional connection (whether we are aware of it or not). In one-night stands or casual sex, the spiritual and emotional aspects have nowhere to go. This wouldn't be a problem if we were merely biological animals with no soul or spirit. However, this is not the case, as we are spiritual creatures contained within physical bodies. Our spiritual selves can feel at the mercy of our humanness, but it's this very humanness that gives expression to our souls.

Every sexual encounter you have that is devoid of any emotional component or is with someone with whom you have no desire to deepen your connection, is an avoidance of feelings and a desperate attempt to remain emotionally numb. When anyone—male or female—is feeling powerless or unworthy, he or she has a radar that detects those who are feeling equally unlovable. The "charge" that is felt when the two connect is interpreted as sexual attraction, and off they go for a superficial roll in the hay. What has really occurred is an intense need to use and/or exploit another person to escape frightening feelings of inadequacy. Even if only for a short while, we need to use the other person to create relief from our inner pain. Each partner represents two sides of a coin, and each uses the other for the same reasons. When interest is limited to satisfying a temporary craving, sex becomes a symptom of fear and low self-esteem, rather than a cure for it.

ONSM is repulsed by women who feel good about themselves. Self-confident, balanced, and whole females hold little attraction for him because he can't find weaknesses to exploit. Like a psychic vampire, he needs insecure blood donors. Our ONSM has his work cut out for him, as he is constantly on the prowl to find his powerless counterpart in order to take from her, no matter how briefly, control, power, and self-worth.

Contrast the motivations and qualities of the one-night stand to those found in a long-term relationship (LTR). In a LTR the complexity of the individual is acknowledged. Each partner cares about the hopes, fears, conflicts, and triumphs of the other. Neither uses the other to feel better about him- or herself. They are spiritually, mentally, and physically on the same page. They also support each other, forgive past mistakes, and allow for human fragility in their relationship. This kind of spiritual union or alliance weathers changes and time, because the focus is on the spiritual part of a person (who they really are), rather than a set of temporary characteristics (what they appear to be).

Blocks and Obstacles to Relationships

Sometimes it may seem as if your (or his) personality or ego is standing in the way of a partnership of any depth, but in fact this is not the case. Your personality is created by your spirit as a tool for your enrichment. The problem with personality is that it is influenced externally. It is shaped and molded by the environment as a tree is gnarled by the wind. Your personality can actually be remarkably adept at staying in communication with your spirit. We need our personalities to understand what it is to suffer hardships, which in turn develops compassion and understanding. All great leaders know first what it is to serve.

Attachment to outcomes

Searching for a hero and falling in love with the idea of someone, rather than the real person, encourages us to become attached to certain outcomes. Much pain and suffering results when reality doesn't fit with fantasy. When things don't turn out as expected, disappointment is the result. Disappointment means we had expectations. Having preconceived expectations is inherently manipulative. Attachment to specific outcomes lead to attempts to control, and attempts to control alienate partners.

Unrealistic expectations

Trying to fit a square peg into a round hole is another lesson in futility. If your guy thinks that marriage is akin to a prison sentence at San Quentin and children are the torture, you, as a wedding planner and earth mother who wants a house full of rosy-cheeked cherubs in red pajamas, are not going to be happy. Holding on to the relationship with a stranglehold won't make him change, but it will waste your time and energy. Unrealistic expectations are the mother of all disappointments.

Poor self-image

We project our own fears onto our relationships. When we are feeling badly about ourselves, separation is seen as abandonment, personal independence is seen as terrifying, and even human frailties are seen as personal attacks. Relationships tend to mirror our internal worlds. What I criticize in my partner is frequently what I dislike in myself. When we resolve our own inner problems it is remarkable how our relationships transform naturally.

A dissatisfied mind

The root of most relationship unhappiness is a dissatisfied mind—dissatisfied, because we look at the glass of love and life as half empty rather than half full. Although staying in this positive and optimistic mindset sounds simple, it is far from an easy thing to do. Most of us start out on life's path as idealistic and hopeful, only to be disillusioned as we discover the cruel and insensitive side of life. However, each moment of each day we can choose whether to view ourselves as victims or victors, blessed or blasted. By intending to be happy and focusing on the bright side of any disappointment, we will greatly increase our chances of finding, nurturing, and sustaining the relationship of our dreams.

The Biochemistry of Love: Dopamine, Prolactin, and Oxytocin

Thanks to the limbic system that lies directly beneath the rational neocortex of our brain, we do not choose who to fall in love with. That oh-so-blissful feeling of being in love (along with sex and desire) is produced by a complex soup of neurotransmitters, hormones, and other chemicals in our brains. The limbic system, or "primitive brain," is the origin of emotions, drives, desires, and impulses. It is also where the feeling of being in love begins. As in the spiritual realm, every biological effect has a biological cause. In this case, the cause is neurochemicals, and the effect is sleepless nights and those butterflies in your stomach.

Dopamine

Among all the neurochemicals, dopamine is *the* mega hormone that activates your reward and pleasure centers. Dopamine is released when we engage in activities that further our survival. Sex, food, taking risks, achieving goals, or even drinking water all increase dopamine, and dopamine "turns on" our reward center. In fact, you can thank dopamine for every craving, obsession, compulsion, or addiction you experience. The more dopamine you release the more your reward center is activated, and the more your reward centers are activated the more you want to revisit the pleasure you have just enjoyed.

A good example is food. We get a much bigger blast of dopamine from eating high-calorie foods than we do from low-calorie foods. It's why we choose cherry cheesecake over broccoli. You are not really craving cake, a winning blackjack hand, or a mind-blowing sex session; in actuality, what you are craving is the dopamine that is released with these activities. Dopamine is your reward, and not really the item or activity itself. All addictions increase dopamine; that is why they are addictive. Money, sex, shopping, and gambling can all be addictive for this reason. It's not a stretch to see how powerful this granddaddy of all hormones can be in your love life.

Despite its involvement in pleasure and excesses, dopamine isn't a bad chemical. In fact, it is absolutely necessary for our survival. It is when there is an imbalance that it gets our attention. Due to the euphoria produced, high levels of dopamine are responsible for addictions, sexual fetishes, risky behavior, and compulsive activities. When it is deficient, just the opposite results, with depression, lack of ambition, low libido, and sleep problems. Basically, dopamine is essential for us to feel motivated, satisfied, pleasured, rewarded, and loved. When you crave a colossal double cheeseburger with fries or that sexy person you met last night, it is really the dopamine fix you're looking for, not the burger or the guy. You can see how dopamine can affect our partnerships.

People use all kinds of external means to manipulate their dopamine levels. The desire to recreate the experience that produced such a potent "high" is a strong motivator! Orgasm is the biggest blast of dopamine naturally available to us. Scientists have studied patterns in the orgasmic brain and found that they resemble those produced by a heroin rush. Dopamine is, hands down, the most addictive substance you produce. Orgasms and addictions have two things in common: They both produce an initial pleasurable experience, which is then followed by an unpleasant comedown or hang-over. What goes up must come down. It is a fact of biology that body systems must return to *homeostasis*, or balance.

What goes up and down in this case is your dopamine. This can play havoc with your moods and the way in which you perceive your partner. With conventional sex and frequent orgasms we are continually going in and out of these dopamine extremes. Considering the behaviors associated with high and low dopamine may help explain how one's lover can do a Jekyll and Hyde transformation. But, it gets better.

Prolactin

The ups and downs of your dopamine levels are only part of the story. After orgasm, dopamine levels drop sharply and we lose interest, at least temporarily. If the dopamine rapidly shoots up again, we'll be back in the sack in no time. Biology's mission now is to stop us from obsessively having sex and place our attention elsewhere instead—eating, sleeping, going to our jobs, taking out the trash, and so forth. To do this, your brain releases another chemical after orgasm called prolactin. Prolactin relaxes the body, which in turn interprets the feeling as a need for sleep. Similar to dopamine, prolactin is not a bad chemical; it is the anti-stress/relaxation hormone responsible for blissful states similar to meditation.

If dopamine is the green light, prolactin is the red light. The dopamine pumps you up and the prolactin winds you down. Prolactin and dopamine are the yin and yang of sex. This rise-and-fall pattern produces a dopamine-prolactin roller coaster of highs and lows, and this roller coaster can wreak havoc with our partnerships.

Most people have not studied the biology of brain chemistry, and therefore do not make this connection of cause and effect. When couples start to lose interest in each other, it may be that they are only experiencing this post-orgasmic "hangover." The symptoms of elevated prolactin levels are decreased sex drive, weight gain, depressed mood, and even hostility. This dopamine-prolactin switch may also explain the dreaded "hump-and-dump syndrome" (the approach-retreat behavior of men, pre- and post-sex) that women often complain about. The result of this chemical roller coaster on your man is that, during the dopamine-prolactin comedown, he may be irritable and interpret your requests as demands. You, on the other hand, may feel needy, and interpret your partner's behavior as uncaring. Although it is not known exactly how long prolactin surges remain in the human system after orgasm, laboratory rats that were injected with prolactin showed its presence in their bloodstreams up to 14 days later. Who knew that the mind-boggling sex you enjoyed during the weekend could be the reason you are bummed out on Monday and Tuesday?

While this dopamine-prolactin hangover is in effect, our rational cerebral cortexes struggle to explain the relationship disharmony. Orgasm is natural, but it may also be natural for both men and women to "sour" on their mates or suddenly find their spouses unattractive, irritating, and/or completely unreasonable. When this occurs a couple enters another phase of their relationship when the romance begins to fade and they begin to perceive each other in a different—actually, more realistic—way. This is when many relationships end.

Curiously, many relationships don't end due to a stale partnership. Reacting to a temporary state created by a medley of brain chemicals can be the real cause. Mark, 32, puts it this way: "I think I've lost count of how many lovers I've had, but it's a lot. I don't understand it, I lose interest in all of them sexually so quickly and some of these women are really beautiful, too." The reason Mark loses interest is that after he orgasms, he is not getting any further dopamine surge from his partner. No dopamine equals no interest. The thrill is gone, and the partner who just looked like cherry cheesecake now resembles broccoli. Enter a new partner, and the dopamine levels soar rapidly. As if by magic, his blues are gone, and he experiences that charged feeling of anticipation and a sense of excitement and aliveness. He is offered cherry cheesecake once more. So, what does the average person do to offset the "hump-and-dump" doldrums of the post-orgasmic experience?

Oxytocin—A Girl's Best Friend

If the dramatic rise and fall in dopamine levels can break couples apart, oxytocin is the magic elixir that can bind them together—at least initially. Oxytocin is responsible for feelings of unconditional love, nurturing, and affection. Without it, we could not fall in love. The feeling of falling in love is, in reality, a neurochemical stew of adrenaline (the racing heart), dopamine (the sexual desire and cravings), and oxytocin (the warm, loving, "gushy" feelings). Interestingly, oxytocin is the same neurochemical that bonds mothers to their babies.

Women can use their knowledge of oxytocin to level the anti-monogamous playing field. This is the secret that the ancient sages stumbled upon. Making love with lots of affection but no orgasm seems to keep oxytocin levels high. And, unlike dopamine, you don't need an ever-increasing fix of oxytocin to maintain the same warm, fuzzy feelings. This is why being physically affectionate—through hugging, kissing, and caressing, for example—*without* orgasm strengthens relationship bonds. Oxytocin has huge benefits, both emotionally and physically. It reduces cravings, calms, promotes feelings of well-being, increases longevity, and speeds healing. Oxytocin also eases depression due to its antagonism to cortisol, a stress hormone that is a major factor in depression and anxiety. This is why making love without orgasm can be satisfying in a different kind of way. The affection is always there, flowing between you and your partner. When we limit dopamine highs and lows, we encourage more oxytocin receptors and actually rewire our brains, enabling them to get pleasure from a different cocktail of neurochemicals. Now we see why Taoist and tantric sexual practices teach and encourage orgasm without ejaculation. Understanding the power of oxytocin suggests how sexual relationships can heal.

Understanding how these brain chemicals work has also begun to unravel the behavioral dynamics of falling in love. When researchers injected oxytocin into the brains of mammals, they preferred familiar partners to unfamiliar partners. Dopamine and its post-orgasmic hangover foster promiscuity, whereas oxytocin imparts a preference for familiarity and monogamy. Its positive effect on men is that it increases sexual receptivity, counteracts impotence, and encourages bonding. Researchers have come up with what they think is the "recipe" for falling in love. Being slightly unavailable or playing hard to get works, because it is the trigger that releases the love hormones. That feeling of being in love is really a complex mix of brain chemicals triggered when your affection is returned somewhat, but not completely. Apparently, absence does make the heart grow fonder. The ingredient of anticipation must also be involved: Your admirer must believe that his love will be returned completely someday,

although only partially today. This explains why "nut magnets" attract nuts. When we act disinterested, but show some
interest by trying to be friendly, it fans the embers of an
admirer's already fiery heart.

Scheherazade and the 1001 Nights

10

But when it was midnight Scheherazade awoke and began to recite some delectable stories to while away the latter night. The King who chanced to be sleepless was pleased.

—Sir Richard Francis Burton,
The Nights

Some of the richest and most colorful stories concerning relationships have emerged from the cradle of civilization, and can be found in the Persian *Hezar-afsana*, or *Thousand Myths* (c. 800–900 AD). From this collection compiled by many authors, scholars, and translators comes such favorites as *The Book of a Thousand Nights and a Night*, and *1001 Arabian Nights*.

The timeless stories that comprise these "thousand myths" center on a Persian king named Shahryar and his wife, Scheherazade. One of the most famous accounts of the couple was immortalized in Sir Richard Francis Burton's translation, *1001 Arabian Nights*. After discovering his wife's infidelity, King Shahryar began to marry a succession of young women, only to execute them the next day (can anyone say "psychopath"?). Anyway, according to Burton's translation, eventually the king's prime minister was forced to offer his own daughter, the beautiful and well-educated Scheherazade. She marries the king, but, aware of her coming fate, she devises a clever plan.

She begins to tell her husband intriguing stories of exotic lands and passionate adventures each night. But, she never finishes her story until the next evening. Each elaborate and colorful tale is even more exciting than the previous one, always leaving the king in suspense. King Shahryar is compelled to keep Scheherazade alive in order to hear the conclusion of her stories. And so it went for 1,001 nights.

In *The Nights*, Burton describes this resourceful and intriguing young woman thusly: "[Scheherazade] had perused the books, annals and legends of preceding Kings, and the stories, examples and instances of by gone men and things.... She had collected a thousand books, perused the works of great poets, studied philosophy, arts and sciences; she was pleasant and polite, wise and witty, well read and well bred." It apparently saved her life.

Some of the more famous fables Scheherazade spins during these spellbinding nights are *Aladdin's Wonderful Lamp*, *The Seven Voyages of Sinbad the Sailor*, and the tales of *Ali Baba's Forty Thieves*. In addition to these popular classics, her nightly tales included captivating love stories, dramatic tragedies, delightful comedies, classical poems, and exciting erotica. According to the ancient manuscripts, after 1,001 of these well-told tales the Sultan king relents. After keeping her alive and eagerly anticipating each new story, the king had not only been entertained, but wisely educated in morality and kindness by Scheherazade, who became his cherished queen.

What constituted a cliffhanger in the times of Scheherazade may not appeal to you personally, but a wise woman will note her technique. The lesson for the modern female is to cultivate your own richly layered Self and keep your "king" curious about your sequels! Ladies who don't disclose everything and keep a little mystery surrounding themselves remain fascinating to the men who love them.

One of the reasons that Scheherazade was so clever is that girls of her time would have been educated in what the Kama Sutra called the 64 Arts. The aim of the 64 Arts was not merely to be a good partner, but to be a skillful, playful, and intelligent woman. The Kama Sutra also admonishes boys to understand the female nature, and the importance of enlightening sensual moods and intimacy. The ancient Indians showed great attention to the details of aromas, lighting, music, food, drink, and tactile sensations before the sexual act began. The 64 Arts to accomplish are:

- Vocal music—notes, rhythm, tempo.
- Musical instruments—percussion, strings, flute.
- Dancing—hand and body movements, expression.
- Drawing—writing styles, art techniques, likenesses.
- Paper cutting—stencils for patterns.
- Making couches out of flowers or colored rice on the ground.
- Arranging flower bouquets.
- Making stains and dyes for the body, teeth, and garments.

- Creating mosaics and stained glass.
- Bed arranging, carpets, and cushions.
- Playing on musical bowls or glasses filled with water.
- Water spitting and spewing games.
- Using charms, drugs, alchemy, and mantras.
- Making garland—trimming and decorating.
- Making crowns and head ornaments.
- Dressing, adornment, and jewelry.
- Making ear ornaments of ivory or mother of pearl.
- Preparing perfumes.
- Making jewelry.
- Learning hypnosis, astrology, and divination.
- Learning magic and tantric sexual skills.
- Performing manicures.
- Mastering the culinary arts.
- Making beverages.
- Sewing and needlework.
- Making lace from yarn or thread.
- Solving conundrums, enigmas, and verbal puzzles.

- Completing quotations.
- Mastering riddles and utilizing formulas.
- Bookbinding.
- Telling stories.
- Quoting the classics in answering questions.
- Making cane baskets and cane furniture.
- Woodworking—lathe detailed.
- Building and architecture—carpentry.
- House furnishing and decoration.
- Expert knowledge of stones and gems.
- Mixing and polishing metals—mineralogy.
- Valuing the shape and color of stones.
- Knowledge of mines and quarries.
- Horticulture—gardening and care of trees.
- Raising and training fine horses for battle.
- Teaching parrots and other birds to talk.
- Learning massage and the care of the body and hair.
- Using sign language, cipher, and symbolism.
- Changing the forms of words when speaking.
- Learning multiple foreign languages and dialects.
- Decorating carriages with flowers.

- ∞ Observing omens and signs.
- ∞ Learning manual dexterity and fabricating simple machines.
- ∞ Developing the memory.
- ∞ Alternate reciting of texts, multitasking.
- ∞ Learning puns and jokes.
- ∞ Knowledge of dictionaries and vocabularies.
- ∞ Composing poems and prose.
- ∞ Learning literary forms.
- ∞ Learning the tricks of cheating.
- ∞ Learning the art of disguise.
- ∞ Learning the art of gaming, gambling, and using dice.
- ∞ Learning the game of chess.
- ∞ Learning about children's games, dolls, and toys.
- ∞ Mastering good manners, the rules of society, and the art of greetings.
- ∞ Learning the rule of success, the art of war, and battle strategies.
- ∞ Achieving physical fitness—flexibility and gymnastics.

As they showed proficiency in each of these arts, I wonder if these women were awarded badges as girl scouts are. Although it is impressive in its eclecticism, this list would make one monstrous liberal arts curriculum!

Purposeful Loving: Creating Lasting Love Connections

11

*I*f statistics are correct, in the majority of relationships, "until death do us part" is neither actual nor practical. The idea that marriage should be for life is many times neither realistic nor reality. Some relationships will indeed last for a lifetime, however others end quite naturally once the reason for the coupling is completed. Unfortunately, when a relationship ends, it rarely ends on a happy or congenial note, especially when one party wants to split and the other doesn't. The volume knob of passion is turned all the way up in such cases. Family, coworkers, and friends all expect a grievous deed such as infidelity or some kind of abuse in order to justify the breakup. In reality, though, many couples split up because of feelings, not crimes that require a restraining order. "For better or for worse" worked well in a time when the average adult died before age 30; however, as longevity increases, so does the likelihood of personal evolution and change.

Contrary to the patriarchal religious idea that a marriage union should never be dissolved, rational thought counters that a partnership should never become a prison. Spiritual partners stay together as long as they are both in harmonious agreement about the relationship. Whether single, married, or somewhere in between, you can begin practicing healthier ways of relating with partners. Becoming successful in love is about having a certain mindset. What's happening in you is much more important than what's happening around you. Sometimes the simplest truths are the most powerful.

You will magnetize yourself to men who share your spiritual intentness, which will set the stage for you to love the true person, and not merely a set of physical and personality characteristics, which are capricious and will quite naturally change. Because every thought is an intention, examining the underlying nature of any relationship is critical to understanding how to sustain it. Seeing your partner through the eyes of love instead of through the lens of expectations, automatically elevates your relationship to a higher plane. Which side of you is orchestrating your relationships, personality/ego or soul/spirit?

Personality/ego result in:	Soul/spirit result in:
Fear	Love
Anger	Agreement
Resentment	Forgiveness
Jealousy	Acceptance
Manipulation	Sincerity
Bad Intent	Good Intent
Hurt	Contentment
Vengeance	Gratitude
Hate	Joy
Judgement	Justice

There are really only four hard-and-fast rules in spiritual relationships:

1. Always follow your own spiritual path. You will begin to attract men who share your spiritual inclinations (and who will hopefully be pursuing their own).

2. Exist in the present time and relate to your partner in the here and now. Stop formulating expectations for the future, as expectations are the mother of all disappointments. You can't control the future and should only learn from the past.

3. Be grateful. Showing gratitude is a powerful, love-based behavior. Always look for and acknowledge the fine points of your partner. Admiring his finer qualities will make him want to be even more of these things.

4. Be clear. Be straightforward and ask for what you need. Most men aren't psychic (although some are), and it is important that you communicate what you want in clear-cut terms. Your man wants to please you, and although he won't slay a beast for the evening meal, it is important that he feels that he meets your needs in other ways.

For Better or for Worse: The Consequences

When we fail to take responsibility for our choices, the result is low self-esteem. The "Cinderella complex" (or "savior searching," as it is sometimes called) is an attempt to escape painful feelings and emotions. When you are a part of the cause, but do not accept personal responsibility for the effect, the resulting powerlessness is the price you will pay for taking this easy way out.

Marcy describes her current husband as a hero because he rescued her from a life of abuse and violence. After living with a drug addicted and brutal man, she turned to the bachelor next door to clean up the mess and solve her troubles after her disturbed husband committed suicide. Marcy and her two children immediately moved in with him and they eventually married. Years later, Marcy is very often unhappy and depressed. Life overwhelms her and she takes everything personally. She's always down about one thing or another—her health, her job, her dying cat, a sick relative. You name it, she's bummed about it.

Marcy is unhappy because she has never taken responsibility for her life or for her own happiness. Whether it's leaving an abusive husband or finding happiness with a new one, she is like a leaf blowing in the wind. Marcy is dependent in a passive-aggressive way, and she covertly manipulates through the practice of people pleasing. By this she hopes to win the favor of those around her. No wonder she feels powerless.

Curtain Calls

Significant people come into our lives at appointed times for specific reasons. This ushers in the phenomena of the karmic "curtain call." When two souls reconnect later in life, the results can be life changing. These kinds of karmic rendezvous strongly suggests a soul mate or twin soul connection. With bonds much deeper than mere physical attraction or a lust-driven driven one-night stand, these are deep relationships that have really never ended.

Rob and Mia went to the same high school in a small rural town. The two became romantically involved, but after high school they began dating other people and the two eventually lost touch with each other. Through the years, Robert tried to find Mia, pressing fellow classmates for her whereabouts. "I looked everywhere for her," he recalls, "but I finally became discouraged and withdrew. I was devastated, but I went on."

When Mia and Rob finally met up at their class reunion it was like they had never parted. The old feelings came back immediately, and it was a tense evening as the two of them tried to hide their obvious attraction and include Marcy, Rob's wife, in the conversation. The evening became even more uncomfortable when Marcy was approached by a guest who asked her if Mia and Rob were married. The chemistry between Rob and Mia was so impossible to hide that Mia politely declined Rob and Marcy's invitation to join them for breakfast the next morning.

Within the early "puppy love" that elders downplay and dismiss as youthful folly lies the seeds of a powerful connection to be continued at a future date. When early partners or teenage loves reconnect, these reunions are surprisingly successful. When reunited again, their separation rate is far lower than the norm. Why is this? Is there a magic formula that explains the endurance of love through the years? In the formative years between 10 and 25, familiar souls tend to group together. Puppy love or adolescent crushes are much more significant than most people realize. Males and females who grow up together, sharing friends, hobbies, schools, and experiences, bond in a special way.

These reunions are frequently the real thing, and can end happily ever after if both of the lost lovers are unattached. However, despite the sunny outlook for these rekindled romances, there is also a shadow side. These attachments are forged on both the biological hormones of adolescence and powerful spiritual bonds. Due to the consummate power of these long-lost love connections, current relationships can be threatened. Lost-love reunions may stay forever unexplored, or they can end existing partnerships. So, when you get that first e-mail from a childhood friend or high school sweetheart, consider carefully before proceeding. Remember: always use the EWO (eyes wide open) principle.

Modern networking abilities made possible by the Web are reuniting more and more first loves and high school sweethearts. Whether it's through a class reunion or Internet search, old flames can ignite a powder keg of emotions.

Forgiveness: Legacies, Skeletons, and Getting Over It

12

Tumultuous relationships are usually saturated with past karma. Intense, passionate, consuming, and occasionally obsessive, these pairings can span lifetimes. To choose one of these high-drama meetings takes courage and is the astral signature of urgently needed spiritual growth. Although one of these can age you 10 years, they do develop character and are catalysts to some serious soul development. The excruciating sting of rejection strikes at the very heart of one's soul, but all passing flames in the wind serve to make us who we are. In actuality, our most bitter disappointments and worst experiences are many times our greatest assets. However, with our present cultural emphasis on the physical, mental, and emotional sides of relationships, few are aware of or know how to repair their spiritual sides. You can start right now by allowing forgiveness to replace any feelings of resentment or anger from hurtful, negative relationships.

We never stop loving those whom we have truly loved. Every past attachment serves as part of a greater purpose or a bigger picture. You would not be who and where you are in this life if you were still with that person, and you could not be who and where you are if he or she hadn't crossed your path. This attitude of relativity seems simple enough, but the inability to forgive is at the core of what prevents many from being receptive to a true soul mate. Remember that you have to intensely love another person in order to intensely hate that person, as well. Complacency is the holy grail of the obsessive love crowd and is a signpost of healing. Relationships generally end when the lessons involved have been learned. If your spiritual connection is strong with someone because there is a great deal of shared past history, and the relationship is severed, the loss can feel unbearable.

The romantic mind is akin to a muddy glass of water; our disappointments are the impurities (the mud), which can be removed to reveal our true, pure nature. Happiness is our birthright, but it is also a conscious choice. By being mentally stuck in the past you remain firmly anchored to it. We eliminate the blocks to intimacy and emotional afflictions by consciously and deliberately cultivating compassion, tolerance, and, most of all, forgiveness. By freeing our minds of past bitterness, disappointment, and dissatisfaction, we become spiritually open and ready to love again. You alone decide, at every moment of every day, whether to carry the emotional weight of the past into your future.

We all make mistakes; it's only human. But when you hold on to a grudge it eats away at your sense of peace and serenity. Bitterness is a toxic companion that will consume from the inside out. It eats away at your very soul. There is nothing like disappointment to illustrate the painful effect of expectations and being attached to a specific outcome. Expectations are an attempt to manipulate, and being disappointed is proof positive that you did indeed hold certain expectations. The greatest power we have is over ourselves. We will repeat relationships until the lessons are learned and we can let them go. Take the road to yourself and write your own love script. The metaphysical approach to love may be just the perceptual shift you need in order to move closer to the love relationship you truly desire.

Forgiveness is the first step on the path to improving your love karma. Don't let your past weigh you down. Awareness leads to understanding, and understanding allows forgiveness. Let go of the past. Realize that your thoughts and intentions create your future romantic reality. Realizing this can be sobering enough to cut the karmic cord for good. Right now, take that step: Think of the person who has hurt you the most—the one who is on your eternal shit list, the deadbeat con artist who cleaned out your savings account, ruined your reputation, and got you fired from your job before saying adios to you and junior. That's the person you must start with. Until you truly forgive him (which involves relinquishing all expectations), there will be a karmic road map to nowhere with your name on it. This toxic cargo in your spirit must be emptied in order to be able to hold, or be filled by, the love you crave—a soul partnership with another.

So find a quiet place, maybe lying in bed in the dark. Picture this person who has consumed so much of your energy for so long, and consciously send him warm feelings. Say, "I forgive you completely and wish you nothing but good things." Concentrate intensely, and communicate right then and there your forgiveness to that person. Make him *feel* you release the bitterness, and send healing love his way. This breaks the karma and the bond between you. This releases you to attract the kind of relationship you want. If you have zeroed in on the real thorn in your side, you may have to make several attempts to be able to fully release the anger (which is really fear) that keeps you in mental bondage. Number one: forgive yourself and anyone else involved. Forgiving them is for you; don't think it is letting anyone off the hook. The law of karma is fair. Whether you call it "cause and effect," "what goes around comes around," or "reaping and sowing" is immaterial—the concept is a universal truth. All actions have effects. Forgive, and refuse to let guilt or resentment sabotage your love life any more. Then make better choices in love and organize your efforts to have a partnership that brings you a deep and soulful joy.

The Bottom Line

Experience has a price, and that price is paid in karmic spades every time we suffer emotional pain. However, when we finally decide to learn from our past, it becomes our teacher and friend rather than our accuser. The cornerstone for good love relationships is spiritual agreement. The universal law of attraction states that if romantic happiness is the desired effect, our job is to identify and then create the cause that will produce the effect—the love—we seek. The cause is the intent to create the effect. Indeed, as James Allen writes in *As a Man Thinketh*, "The soul attracts that which it secretly harbors, that which it loves, and also that which it fears." Our consciousness is the stronger power, and can override subconscious choices once it becomes aware of them.

Don't be wishy-washy and uncertain about love! Don't say things such as, "Well, I'm going to try this relationship and see how it goes. Maybe it will work out, maybe it won't." The universe itself works on the intent principle. Make a clear, committed decision, and it will open the universal romantic floodgates, bringing you all the love you need, sometimes in seemingly impossible ways.

After you declare your intention to find love, use patience and faith to wait for the resources and synchronizations to arrive. If your love path seems too complicated or difficult and you don't like what you see, change your intentions and declare what you want. For example, if you declare your intent to find the love of your life, soon you may begin to see all sorts of synchronicities related to spirituality. This may seem to have nothing to do with romance whatsoever. But this is not a pointless coincidence. It is a sign that the path to romance first requires you to improve your spiritual consciousness. If you hook up with a life partner before your spiritual energy and consciousness has reached a certain level, there may be problems. But if you first cultivate your own happiness and spiritual Self, that love will manifest in a positive rather than negative way. Forgiveness is the essential ingredient that opens the doors to freedom and true romantic happiness.

Affirmations That Work: Meditation, Guided Imagery, and Accessing Your Subconscious

13

Meditation can be described as any activity in which you control your attention in order to achieve a relaxation response. Meditation bridges the mind-body connection. Breath control and practices such as prayer and mindful meditation activate the vagus nerve, which leads to a reduction in heart rate, respiration, and blood pressure. Not only are there tremendous physical benefits (such as the de-stressing and antiaging effects) from meditative practices, but also great spiritual and emotional benefits as well.

Physically speaking, our brain has four basic metabolic levels, as demonstrated by the four different brain waves: Beta waves are functioning when our conscious mind makes decisions; alpha waves are functioning when our subconscious mind seeks the truth and does not rationalize; theta waves are functioning when our unconscious mind keeps involuntary bodily functions operating; and delta waves are functioning when our superconscious is involved in higher thought or spiritual communion.

The answers to our most basic questions—who am I? what is my life's purpose?—are stored in the memories of our subconscious. This is where we are authentic and real, just as we came into this life—stripped of all excuses, rationalizations, and half-truths. The most effective way to get in touch with our spiritual essence, guides, and counselors is by way of meditation. Not only can we learn an infinite amount about our true motivations, but we can also make positive and helpful suggestions to our subconscious. This is imperative, because your subconscious mind is the "goal striver" of your psyche. If you don't give it positive goals and direction by way of conscious choice, it will take its own, often convoluted path. This is why conscious intent and the words we speak are so powerful.

There are numerous forms of meditation and each has its own characteristic method, but all share the goal of relaxation, mindfulness, and accessing the higher vibrational brainwave states (alpha, theta, and delta).

Transcendental Meditation

Transcendental meditation, also known as TM, is one of the most popular types of concentration meditation. It is a stress-reducing and healing practice in which your attention is focused on one thing, such as the rhythm of your breathing, a mantra, or a phrase that is continually repeated. TM is part of a healing system called *Maharishi Ayur-Veda*, introduced to the West by Maharishi Mahesh Yogi. Meditating twice daily for 20 minutes develops a state of restful alertness.

Mindfulness Meditation

Mindfulness or insight meditation involves intentional, nonjudgmental, moment-to-moment awareness. Similar to its cousin, TM, mindful meditation begins with focused attention, but expands to observe feelings, sensations, intuition, and thoughts, ideally without judging or analyzing. Stressful situations are mitigated with a mindful response rather than a mindless reaction to events. By learning to live and to love in the moment (which means releasing expectations), we can avoid a great deal of unnecessary conflict and pain.

Om, or *aum*, is a Sanskrit syllable used frequently in meditation as a mantra. A meditation mantra spoken repeatedly becomes a chant, which in turn influences thought by means of sound vibration. *Om* is said to be the sound symbol for the earth and creation, and the universal sound vibration of existence. Eastern masters believe it is possible to become one with the source of all things by uttering this sound (the long O ending with the prolonged, vibrating M through closed lips). Modern health practitioners also endorse this technique to alleviate stress and release the neurotransmitters responsible for elevated moods.

Guided Imagery

Imagining relaxing and healing images to aid relaxation is the sum and substance of guided imagery. Using your senses and imagination, guided imagery promotes healing and reduces anxiety. In a relaxed state of concentrated attention, ideas and suggestions have a powerful impact on the mind. Deep meditation is the secret to accessing your spiritual Self. For answers, for guidance, and for direction toward your higher purpose, it's all there. All of these answers are contained in the precious storehouse of your own subconscious. Accessing the subconscious alpha waves of our brains by way of meditation allows access to our true Selves. We "remember" the reason for our present existence and the Source from whence we came.

We all have many questions about our individual destinies, and listening for the answers is the key. They don't come as a sudden flash of lightning, but can only be heard by getting to know ourselves, finding out what we really want, and believing in ourselves. Learn to listen to your intuition, the inner spiritual voice of your true Self. This is where the answers to your success and happiness reside.

Positive Affirmations That Work

Find a quiet place where you can sit comfortably and undisturbed for at least 20 minutes. Sit with your legs crossed, eyes closed, shoulders relaxed, and hands resting comfortably on your thighs. As you relax, begin to notice your breath. Just relax and notice it. Focus on your breath going out and in. Picture your ideal Self, the you that feels proud and powerful, and yet is lovable and vulnerable at the same time. Visualize your beloved or ideal partner, as well. During your daily meditation, bring this picture to mind and feel yourself there. When you become accustomed to entering deep alpha wave states or higher, you might even want to visualize sitting in a beautiful place—perhaps a park or by the ocean—

and have a conversation with your ideal partner. Go ahead and tell him your dreams and feelings and hopes and fears; but then, expect to listen to what your new friend has to say back to you. The insights could be extraordinary.

Recite the following positive affirmations to yourself during your meditation or make up your own—as long as they contain only positive self-talk and are love based.

Positive healing affirmations

I love and accept myself completely.

I release all painful parts of my past and am starting anew.
I forgive all those who have hurt me.

I make time for myself in order to listen to my inner voice.

I am a loving person and attract only loving people.

I will pursue my dreams and am achieving personal goals.

I view challenges as opportunities.

I am aware of how my body is feeling and listen to its signals.

I am hopeful and optimistic; I expect a good outcome.

The only boundaries for me are those I place on myself;
I can make my own dreams come true.

I intend to create a happy romantic future.

When I notice an effect, I look for the cause.

I listen to my intuition and trust my gut instincts; I have
faith in myself.

I make others laugh and look at life with good humor.

I stay present in the current moment; I don't anticipate the
future and only learn from the past.

I am successful and self-confident.

Everything is relevant; I find beauty all around me.

I have an abundance of self-esteem and am learning new
things about my true Self every day.

I am grateful for the good things in my life.

Traditional Zen Meditation

If you have a little more time, why not learn and practice some traditional Zen meditation. Find a quiet, comfortable spot—neither too hot nor too cold, or too bright or too dark. Place a cushion on the floor, preferably on top of a thin pad, blanket, or pillow. Meditation cushions, pads, pillows, sofa cushions, or rolled-up blankets work well for meditation at home. Meditating in a comfortable chair or on a low bench will also work.

The traditional sitting postures are the full lotus posture, the half lotus posture, the quarter lotus posture, the Burmese posture, and the kneeling posture. In each position, the spine is kept straight and the chin is tucked in. The head should be in line with the shoulders. The hands are held close to the body, palms open and up, and with the left hand resting on top of the right. The joints of the two middle fingers should rest on top of one another, and the tips of the thumbs should be lightly touching. The eyes should normally be half closed. However, if you're uptight or anxious, you might want to start with your eyes completely closed to help calm your mind. If you become sleepy during meditation, open your eyes wide to help yourself wake up.

Rest your knees directly on the mat or floor. If you are sitting in a chair, you should sit on the front edge of the chair with your back erect, as described above, with your feet flat on the floor and your legs slightly apart. Once the sitting posture is achieved, rock back and forth a few times to establish your point of balance and a feeling of relaxed stability. Take a few deep breaths, allowing your lungs to expand fully, and then exhale fully. As your breath settles back to a normal rhythm, breathe through your nose with your tongue lightly touching the palate behind your teeth.

Count your breaths. Let all thoughts pass. If thoughts arise, treat them as clouds passing by. Acknowledge them and let them pass. Focus your attention on your breath. Count from one to 10, either as you inhale or exhale, and then start the sequence over. If you follow your breaths, simply put your attention on your breath as you inhale and exhale. When your mind wanders, return your attention to the breathing or the counting. Do not chastise yourself if your attention wanders. The purpose of the mind is to produce thoughts; they are with us always. The idea is to keep returning our attention to our breath or our counting, and our thoughts will settle down naturally. Zen teachers suggest to sit for short periods in the beginning. A good goal to start with would be 10 minutes. Later, as you gain experience and confidence, you can extend the periods up to 20 or 30 minutes. It's a good idea to take a break after 25 or 30 minutes of sitting.

The point of Zen meditation is to discover your true nature and enable you to live a truly mindful life, by experiencing your life in the present moment, in each breath, to the fullest. If you find that Zen meditation is something you'd like to continue with in a group, check to see if there is a teacher or sitting group near you.

Part II

Artha: Happiness, Success, and Prosperity

Just for Fun:
Rate Your Man

14

*Those things that increase passion
should be done first, and those which are
for amusement should be done afterward.*
—Kama Sutra, 7th century BC

My mother tried to teach me to be a
"girlie-girl"—you know, instruction in
sewing, handcrafts, shopping, which
fork to use. However, she never passed
on a single, solitary scrap of usable advice concerning men or dating. So
along my princess path and throughout the years I have bumbled and

stumbled, wondered and blundered through the battlefields of love. In the process, I have devised my own Karmic Keepers or Kickers Rating System (KKRS).

To find out how your beloved rates on the Keepers or Kickers Rating System, answer the following questions in each category as honestly as possible. Choose only one answer. Add up his points as you go along and then total them at the end. With 0 being the worst and 4 being the best, the higher his point score the better your relationship potential.

What book would your guy be most likely to write?

Chardonnay Before Noon (0)

Not All Men Are Fools; Some Are Bachelors (1)

Love Me, Love My Car (2)

The Obscure Scientific Reference Guide to Deep-Sea Sponges (3)

Couple's Guide to Lamaze Childbirth (4)

Where is your guy most likely to eat?

The local soup kitchen. (0)

Any burger drive-thru down Ptomaine Row. (1)

His mom's house. (2)

Anywhere they don't have paper napkins. (3)

Restaurant? Heck no, he'll cook! (4)

How does he feel about animals?

"Where's my hunting rifle?" (0)

"I won a goldfish once at the county fair." (1)

"I'm a cat man, and I love the independent companionship." (2)

"I have one very old dog who's been with me since childhood." (3)

"Crikey! The Australian Zoo has nothing on me! I spend most of my paycheck at Petco." (4)

Where would you most likely find him on his day off?

Taking bong hits with his buddies while in the throes of a beer binge. (0)

Sleeping. (1)

Watching nine uninterrupted hours of televised sports. (2)

Endlessly sorting through new MySpace backgrounds. (3)

With you. (4)

Which of the following terms or phrases would he most likely use to describe his ex?

Dead. (0)

Psychotic. (1)

Needy. (2)

Wasn't meant to be. (3)

A nice person: "We've both moved on, but remain friends." (4)

What is in the back seat of his car right now?

A dead body. (0)

Empty beer cans and fast food trash. (1)

A whole bunch of computer equipment. (2)

Half his wardrobe and toiletries, as he's seldom home. (3)

Some massage oil and a special card for your birthday. (4)

What's your guy's favorite thing to wear?

A diaper. (0)

A pleather loincloth with brass studs and rhinestones. (1)

Whatever he can find that's clean. (2)

The same shorts and Mickey Mouse shirt he's worn for the past five years. (3)

Anything from a tux to jeans; he's comfortable in both. (4)

What's the last sporting event he watched?

A dog fight in his neighbor's garage. (0)

Whatever game his bookie bet on. (1)

The running of the bulls in Spain. (2)

He's more brain than brawn; he doesn't follow sports. (3)

Anything from box seats with you. (4)

Where is your guy's dream home?

Sector 41 of Gamma quadrant 16-B, subsection D. (0)

Anywhere by himself. (1)

His parents' guest house. (2)

Part-time at his place, part-time at yours. (3)

Anywhere with you. (4)

How did he get his scar?

He participated in an ancient fertility ritual. (0)

A gang fight. (1)

His ex. (2)

It's one of many from childhood. (3)

From rescuing, helping, or assisting someone or something. (4)

Which of the following has he lost in the last year:

His will to live. (0)

357 pounds on the new coffee/cigarette diet. (1)

His wallet, keys, cell phone, two credit cards, and a checkbook. (2)

His cool once or twice. (3)

His desire for the dating scene and singles world. (4)

His childhood consisted of:

Alien abductions for painful medical experiments. (0)

Trailer parks, bowling alleys, and paternity tests. (1)

Head injuries from bike rides down Deadman's Hill. (2)

An unconventional family, but overall it was okay. (3)

The best of times, fond memories, and doting parents. (4)

Does he see himself married in the next five years?

No, never, nada, no how, no way. (0)

He thinks that marriage is a ritual invented by those who died at age 20. (1)

His previous marriage left him with more post-traumatic stress than a POW. (2)

He's been toying with the idea. (3)

Yes, he'd like to start a family. (4)

Although the sum of his karma points will tell the whole tale, a guy who scored a 4 on any of the questions deserves some extra kudos. If he scored 4 points on more than three questions, this is a guy who will take care of you and hold your feverish head when you have the flu. Sure his puppy will chew up your best pumps, but he has a heart of gold and plenty of room for you. The answers marked with a score of zero are the ones so dismal that they don't deserve even one point. Hopefully your guy didn't score any zeros, but if he did, do you really want to spend your life with Tommy Chong? Buy him a case of Doritos and say goodbye!

Totaling His Karma Points

Total points from above:____

If your guy scored 35–52 points:

Congratulations, you two are most likely thick as thieves,

and the odds are good that you've made a karmic connection! Your guy has long-term relationship potential, and your relationship is more than just a passing flame. Soul mates are kindred spirits and true helpmates to each other, and that is what you are. The attraction between you is powerful—this could be a relationship that stands the test of time. There is a strong friendship component present here, and couples who are best friends tend to stay together. Although no relationship is perfect, I expect to find you two rolling in a wildflower field or walking hand-in-hand along the shore of a beach somewhere. Congratulations on finding the real deal!

If your guy scored 30–35 points:

Significant people come into our lives at appointed times. It's apparent that you care enough about yourself to have chosen a fairly compassionate man and most likely a good friend as well. Although he is not perfect, this is someone you could very possibly spend your life with. This is a guy who will walk by your side in support and agreement (well, most of the time). It's that other part of the time that you must consider. Relationships that score in this range tend to get stuck in ruts, become distant, or outlive their usefulness. If this happens, it's better to end the partnership on friendly terms, being grateful for the lessons learned.

If your guy scored 20–30 points:

You have gotten mixed up with a slightly selfish, but not disturbed or by any means hopeless, person. Enlightenment and knowledge is the key with this guy. Don't let him get away with bad behavior; he's testing his limits with you. Ask yourself regularly, Is being with him making me a better person? Or could this guy be a poster child for Prozac? You may already have doubts or be wondering what's wrong. Is it him? Is it you? The answer may be neither and both of you. You are two very different people and might make better friends than lovers. Be cautious, and don't invest more of your heart than you can bear to lose.

If your guy scored 14–26 points:

As they say, hope springs eternal, but if your guy falls in this category, his "spring" has probably dried up. Does this guy actually show any interest in your life at all? Can you work with him on mutual goals or plans for the future? Or could your relationship be summed up by the phrase "shock and awe"? At the very least, this guy needs some time (and perhaps a smack to the head) to learn how to treat a lady. Listen to your instincts. Men who score in this range tend to be emotional vampires. This is the kind of guy who makes you want to mark him with exploding ink to warn the next woman.

If your guy scored 10 points or less:

Once in a lifetime something truly awful comes along. To be blunt, this "Mr. Wonderful" has all of the charm of a guy who would circumcise his offspring with a conch shell. Relationships this dismal can turn any normal woman into an irrational basket case in no time. Men who score in this category are prepubescent narcissists, intellectual waste dumps, and complete emotional voids. If a glass of wine and a Valium have become your breakfast, this guy needs to be kicked to the curb. Maybe he'll grow up, get therapy, and work out his issues—or maybe he won't. Either way, forget him. Life's too short to waste with a selfish and senseless Neanderthal such as this. You'll be better off alone.

Cleaning Out Your Romantic Wardrobe

15

*E*very girl develops a collection of "coverings," or karmas, that make up her romantic "wardrobe." I'd like you to go through and weed out, throw out, or pass on those items of clothing—the men in your life—who no longer fit you or are appropriate for you.

Toss list:

1. Too small—petty, stingy, small-minded, miserly men.
2. Too large—narcissistic, vain, or egomaniacal men.

3. Ugly—negative, hateful, prejudiced men.

4. Ripped or torn—broken, damaged, personality-disordered men.

5. Dirty—perverted, sex-addicted, deviant men.

6. Out of style—significantly older or younger men (plus or minus 20 years).

7. Never worn—confirmed bachelors and commitment-phobic men.

8. Faded—drunk, stoned, or substance-addicted men.

9. Missing a button—abnormal or insane men.

10. Stretched out—men with heavy debt, who are financially encumbered, or bankrupt.

Let's look at the problematic wardrobe items one at a time.

1. Too Small

Penny pinchers, tightwads, and cheapskates belong in this category and find themselves at number one on the toss list. Mr. Small suffers from the dreaded "small man syndrome," and is usually touting a particularly paltry peewee (so to speak). He constantly corrects your slightest mistakes even in public, making you feel like a nervous, unintelligent wreck. This is a guy who compensates for his shortcomings by purchasing the biggest truck in town. The next time he tells you that you are too chubby, plain, boring, or stupid, chip away at his boyfriend status, not at your self-esteem.

Frugality can be, and often is, a virtue. It implies that you're being careful, not wasteful, with your resources. However, stinginess is something else entirely. Stinginess is wanting the best for yourself and less for everyone else. Chintzy Chuck (a variety of Mr. Small) makes choices that prove costly to others. He splits meals, buys clothes to wear once and then return, and seldom buys gifts. If a guy doesn't pay on the first date or doesn't leave a tip, it's an early warning sign that you may be lunching with a Mr. Small.

How a man spends or fails to spend his resources is a direct reflection of how generous and giving he is in other areas of his life. Actually, this trait applies to all aspects of a man's character, from how open he is with his feelings to how much love he is able to give. If he never calls because of the "huge phone bill," never wants to go to a nice place because he "can't afford it," or insists on saving gas by walking, even if it's 5 degrees below zero outside, toss the cheapskate.

A cheap man will always be a cheap man, in and out of bed. Stinginess has little to do with how much money a man makes. Stinginess is an attitude. Normal men will push the car before they would ask a date for gas money. If he is a cheapskate now, he will be 10 times worse if you marry him. Mr. Small, as do most ungenerous people, often ends up alone with his money. Don't get stuck with a cheapskate!

Use his own cheap man return policy and exchange this guy for a new model, satisfaction guaranteed!

2. Too Large

Narcissistic, egomaniacal, selfish, self-centered, and vain men belong in this category and find themselves at number two on the toss list. So widespread is this granddaddy of all male personality disorders that it deserves its own special section on the wardrobe toss list. Narcissists respond extremely unfavorably to anything that threatens their idea that they are special or privileged. (That's a nice way of saying they are pubescent jackasses who throw a tantrum if ignored.) Grandiose in thought and behavior, the narcissist's need for admiration, lack of empathy, and hypersensitivity to criticism distinguish him as a giant amongst selfish and asinine men. Common character traits and behaviors include: exaggerated sense of self-importance; expectation of special treatment; exaggeration of achievements and talents; idealization and then rapid devaluation of his partner; and preoccupation with fantasies of brilliance, success, power, beauty, and ideal love.

This infuriating elitist believes that he is special and unique, and should only associate with other special or high-status people. Beware, ye tender ladies—this is the smoothest of the smooth con artists. This damaging man can slip under even the most savvy woman's radar. What makes a relationship with Mr. Too Large so damaging is his exploitative style. He uses women to achieve his own ends, and that's what you'll want on a stick after he gets through with you—his backside.

One of the things that might attract you to him is how quickly he says "I love you," or how soon he wants to marry or commit to you. This is his idealization phase. However, in just a short time he will move into his devaluation phase. Just weeks before you were the love of his life; now you are nagging him into insanity and all he can see are your faults. As soon as he catches you he doesn't want you anymore. The immortal words of Groucho Marx offer an apt description of the narcissist's mind-set: "I refuse to belong to any club that will accept me as a member."

3. Ugly

This man's colors are so unflattering that his personality hue is somewhere between unsightly and hideous. You could say that your personal colors clash in an unflattering way. Ugly men have negative, hateful outlooks on life. Racists, bigots, and just plain mean men belong in this category, and find themselves at number three on the toss list.

As few relationships start on terms other than sweetness and light, it can sometimes be difficult to recognize Mr. Ugly during the early, honeymoon stage of a relationship. A relationship with Mr. Ugly can mean years of heartache, emotional turmoil, and even physical abuse. Getting hooked up with a negative hate-monger can damage your spirit, damage your loved ones, and forever damage the way you feel about love and romance.

Although Arnie Abuser (a version of Mr. Ugly) tends to direct his ill will toward some scapegoat, usually a particular race, religion, or nationality, his toxic waste dump of a soul can also turn on you. If he ever threatens you, hits you, twists your arm, pulls your hair, kicks you, shoves you, or breaks your personal property *even once*, toss him far and fast!

4. Ripped or Torn

Manipulators, players, and psychologically messed-up guys belong in this category, and find themselves at number four on the toss list. A ripped or torn man creates social, emotional, and psychological chaos in a relationship. He has certain permanent patterns of behavior that create this dysfunction. His own personality characteristics he accepts simply as "just the way he is," and does not see them as a problem. Mr. Torn's personality disorder is a coping mechanism learned early in life. Victims of broken or damaged men fill psychologist's offices. Women who survive such relationships end up severely depressed or with their self-esteem permanently damaged, and often end up forming support groups.

When involved in a dysfunctional relationship with a personality-disordered man, you often know something is wrong, but you can't quite put your finger on it. Personality disorders differ, but they all have certain things in common: a disturbed self-image; an inability to have meaningful relationships; a lack of boundaries; and bizarre ways of thinking and of perceiving others. Some common signposts of a ripped or torn man include: self-centeredness ("me, me, me"); a victim mentality (blaming others, society, or the universe for his problems); a lack of accountability (rules don't apply to him); an inability to empathize; exploitive or manipulative behavior; a distorted view of self and others; and an inability to see his behavior as unacceptable or destructive. Following is your travel guide through the land of dysfunctional, disordered men. If you recognize your float along this parade route, please *run*, don't walk, to your nearest relationship exit.

Antisocial Personality Disorder

These guys aren't difficult to spot. Their lack of compassion and inability to restrain their reactions usually repels an emotionally healthy female. However, certain antisocials (such as con men, gigolos, and "master sinisters") are experts at concealing their true selves—for a while, anyway. Completely disregarding others, crossing boundaries, and violating rights are behaviors that characterize the antisocial male.

Specific behaviors to look for include: clashes with law enforcement, lying, the use of aliases, conning others for personal profit or pleasure, impulsiveness, aggressiveness, frequent physical fights or assaults, a disregard for the safety of others, and a lack of remorse. All of these constitute the trademarks of a full-fledged sociopath. Flee and don't look back!

Avoidant Personality Disorder

These men feel woefully inadequate and can be spotted by their extreme sensitivity to criticism, fear of rejection, and desire to be social hermits. Behaviors and character traits to look for include: a resistance to intimacy, a fear of being shamed or ridiculed, extreme feelings of inadequacy, viewing himself as inferior or unappealing, and a reluctance to engage in activities that he fears may prove embarrassing.

Borderline Personality Disorder

If your guy has a scary temper and blows up, or does dangerous things such as driving too fast because he's angry, that temper could soon be turned in your direction. Borderline men respond in an extreme way to any kind of perceived abandonment. Even something as innocent as going to the store without him can send him into a rage. He can be recognized by his rapidly fluctuating moods as well as by his history of changeable and unstable personal relationships. Euphoria versus hopeless doom make his relationships fickle, shallow, and generally of short duration. Behaviors and character traits to look for include: dramatic efforts to avoid real or imagined abandonment; intense interpersonal relationships; an unstable self-image or sense of Self; impulsive spending, sexual activity, and gambling; substance abuse; reckless driving; suicidal behavior, gestures, or threats; chronic feelings of emptiness; and difficulty controlling anger.

Dependent Personality Disorder

This man needs to be taken care of. Pervasive fear leads to excessive "clinging" and an extreme need for you to make the decisions. Fear of separation, submissive behavior, and a marked lack of decisiveness and self-confidence characterize this disorder. Behaviors and character traits to look for include: difficulty making everyday decisions; the need for you to assume responsibility for his life; difficulty expressing disagreement with others; the fear of losing your support or approval; difficulty initiating projects or doing things on his own; and a lack of confidence in his own judgment. The dependent man will go to great lengths to obtain support from you. Here we find the eternal sons who never leave home and the men who stay in impossible or abusive relationships.

Histrionic Personality Disorder

Excessive emotionality and attention-seeking are the calling cards of the histrionic male. These guys exhibit exaggerated and often inappropriate displays of emotional reactions that approach the theatrical—think Richard Simmons in a panic. Behaviors and character traits to look for include: discomfort in situations in which he is not the center of attention; the tendency to consider relationships as more intimate than they actually are; displaying inappropriate or sexually seductive behavior; dramatic expression of emotions; the use of physical appearance to draw attention to himself; and speech that is dramatic, outdated, or metaphoric. The histrionic male will exhibit ridiculous self-dramatization, theatricality, and exaggerated expression of emotions. He is also suggestible and easily influenced by others or circumstances.

Obsessive-Compulsive Personality Disorder

This man is characterized by a preoccupation with orderliness, perfectionism, and interpersonal control. He also obsesses over uncontrollable thoughts or actions, many of which are disturbing. If he turns all of your soup cans in the pantry so that they are all facing in the same direction, or is bankrupting you with his hand soap purchases, you might be dealing with some form of OCPD. Some behaviors and character traits to look for include: perfectionism that interferes with completing projects; rigidly strict standards;

workaholism; and inflexibility about matters of morality, ethics, or values. A preoccupation with details, rules, lists, order, organization, or schedules, to the extent that he loses
the major point of the activity, is also common. This is a guy
who is unable to discard worn out or worthless objects even
when they have no sentimental value to him.

Paranoid Personality Disorder

This guy has an extreme mistrust and suspicion of others. He believes, without reason, that others are exploiting,
harming, or trying to deceive him. He perceives slights and
attacks on himself that are not apparent to others. His overall lack of trust, his tendency to see hidden meanings and
motives, and his unforgiving grudge-holding make him a
particularly nasty companion. Some behaviors and character traits to look for include: suspicions that others are exploiting, harming, or deceiving him; doubts about the loyalty
of friends and family; sees hidden demeaning or threatening intent behind innocent remarks or events; and bears
grudges and is unforgiving of insults, injuries, or slights. This
is the oh-so-fun partner who, without justification, suspects
your every move—your fidelity, your whereabouts, your
motives, and even your chocolate chip cookie recipe. You
name it, he suspects it.

Schizoid Personality Disorder

This guy exhibits a detachment from, and an indifference toward, social relationships and has limited contact with others. He has no real desire for close relationships, including being part of a family. This is a guy who will almost always choose solitary activities, has very little interest in sex, lacks close friends or confidants, and appears cold, indifferent, detached, or dejected. Not exactly Mr. Congeniality, but you aren't likely to encounter him due to his reclusive nature.

Schizotypal Personality Disorder

Extreme perceptual distortions and eccentricities of behavior are the trademarks of the schizotypal personality. Peculiarities of thinking; eccentricities of appearance, behavior, and interpersonal style; and magical thinking, are usually bizarre enough to alarm a watchful female. Some behaviors and character traits to look for include: odd beliefs or bizarre fantasies such as thinking he is Christ, Buddha, some important historic figure, or an alien from another solar system; hallucinations; and speech that is vague, dramatic, or metaphorical. This odd man goes far beyond eccentric and definitely doesn't belong in your romantic closet.

5. Dirty

Compulsive, paraphilic, and sadomasochistic men belong in this category, and find themselves at number five on the toss list. Women sometimes become involved with men who have some form of compulsive sexual behavior (CSB). The reality is that we live in a society that produces people with these sexual dysfunctions. Non-paraphilic compulsive sexual behavior has been called, variously: hypersexuality, hyperphilia, erotomania, perversion, nymphomania, promiscuity, Don Juanism, and sexual addiction. Mr. Dirty will have a pattern of sexual relationships involving lovers who are thought of only as objects to be used. His resume will read something like this: compulsive cruising and multiple partners; fixation on unattainable partners; compulsive autoeroticism (masturbation); compulsive use of porn; compulsive multiple love relationships; and compulsive sexuality within a relationship.

On a darker note, paraphilic compulsive sexual behavior is a much more tangled web of potential problems. The paraphilias are: pedophilia, exhibitionism, voyeurism, sexual masochism, sexual sadism, fetishism, and frotteurism. By nature, paraphilic behavior interferes with a person's feeling of well-being and ability to form or sustain reciprocal love relationships. The most common of these paraphilias (and therefore the one that you have the greatest chance of encountering) is the convoluted world of sadomasochism. Pain is your body's way of telling you that something is wrong, and of telling the brain that damage of some kind is occurring. Those who cannot feel pain or choose to ignore it are at great risk for permanent injury. When you hold your hand above a flame, the pain you feel is your body's way of telling you that if you do not move your hand, the skin tissues will be damaged. Sadomasochism may not be morally wrong or evil, but it is definitely is a stupid thing to do from your body's point of view (more about this in Chapter 18).

Here are some red flags that you might be dealing with someone with CSB:

- ∞ He's preoccupied or obsessed with sexual activity.
- ∞ He engages in sexual activity in response to stress, anxiety, or depression.
- ∞ He's had serious relationship problems as a result of his sexual behavior
- ∞ He engages in what some would consider "deviant" sexual behavior.
- ∞ He constantly searches or scans the environment for a potential sexual partner.
- ∞ His patterns of masturbation are excessive, driven, or dangerous.

- ∞ He spends excessive amounts of time on the Internet viewing pornography.
- ∞ He's had numerous love relationships that were short-lived, intense, or unfulfilling.

All compulsive sexual behavior is a grab for external power, rather than internal, spiritual power. All CSBs and perversions are outward manifestations of a damaged part of the personality calling the shots, rather than the spirit.

6. Out of Style

Significantly older or younger men (plus or minus 20 years), sugar daddies, sultans, and boy toys all belong in this category, and find themselves at number six on the toss list. You may feel that you have more in common with someone significantly older or younger. However, although chronological age is not the only factor in someone's emotional or spiritual maturity, a large age disparity between two people can pose some insurmountable hurdles.

Older man/younger woman

Potential negatives include different energy levels, incompatible sexual drives, and dissimilar interests. It can pose problems if at 10 p.m., the older man is reading *Don Quixote* in bed while his greatly younger partner wants to go out for a late dinner and dancing. Lifestyles can also be a problem.

Take children, for example: he's already raised them, but you may want some of your own someday. Or you may already have children that are still young. Does he want to be a dad again and do all of the "dad things" required? Will he be the only 70-year-old dad at his child's high school graduation (assuming he lives that long)? Another problem is lack of similar interests. He loves the Grateful Dead and Celtic folk music, while your CD case contains Rage Against the Machine and Korn. Once the chemistry wears off, interests tend to grow apart. The older guy looks toward retirement, relaxing, and slowing down, while you may want to start a new business. He wants a golf cart and you want a convertible. In short, there are many mature, wise, secure, appreciative men in their 50s and beyond who would make great mates, but you will be missing out on meeting someone much better suited for you.

Older woman/younger man

Women who date guys that are significantly younger face similar problems. All you want to do after a long day is pop in your yoga video and enjoy a quiet workout. The problem is, Tony the Boy Toy has your TV occupied with his latest PlayStation 3 game. I admit that there are exceptions—couples with an age gap can have wonderful relationships, but it's how closely they relate as spiritual partners that matters. But overall, women who date men closer to their own age fair better and have less to worry about. So go ahead and toss Mr. Out of Style.

7. Never Worn

Confirmed bachelors and commitment-phobes belong in this category, and find themselves at number seven on the toss list. By the time a man hits never-worn status, he will be about as amenable to a committed partnership as he would be to jumping off a bridge. Despite what he says about wanting to find the right woman and settle down, listen carefully—he will tell you himself why his is a dead-end relationship road. The stories he tells about himself are surprisingly cavalier narratives that usually include a list of the many beautiful and talented women who have loved him—all of whom either gave up waiting for him or did something grievous (such as putting on 15 pounds), in which case they were dumped.

"I just haven't found the right girl yet" is Mr. Never Worn's favorite motto. The problem is, he's said this for the last 30 years. He may even let it slip that other women have suggested he is "emotionally dysfunctional" or "narcissistic," or that he might have some commitment issues. Listen carefully to what he says while nostalgically reminiscing about these other women whom he was "very fond of." He will unconsciously describe how you will be treated and what's coming your way.

What he says: "I just haven't found the right girl yet."

Translation: "I've known many 'right girls,' but hedge the issue of commitment in fear that someone better could come along."

What he says: "Don't adjust my knobs; they are perfectly tuned."

Translation: "I've had many people point out that there is something amiss with me, but I have no intention of altering my behavior."

What he says: "I am not very close with my family; I prefer friends of my own choosing."

Translation: "I have trouble 'bonding' due to a dismal childhood, and my 'friends' are primarily women who will be brought into play if and when I need to distance myself from you."

What he says: "I don't know what I'll be doing on_____."
(Fill in major holiday.)

Translation: "I have no intention of spending it with you, and I want to hold it open to pursue plans of my own."

You say: "I love you."

He says: "You poor thing."

Translation: Believe him! He has no capacity for, or intention of, returning your love.

You ask: "Why are you not still with_____?" (Fill in name of last girlfriend.)

He says: "Because the relationship was not moving fast enough for her."

Translation: This man has no intention of settling down with you or anyone. His other relationships ended because they never moved forward.

You still might be tempted to hang in there, but imagine the following scenario. Finally you are at his place. A quick glance around will tell you a great deal. What does his house, apartment, or room remind you of? Does the whole place just scream "don't touch"? Does it look like a museum of relationships past? Are there "trophies" of relationships past strewn about—pictures, articles of women's clothing, jewelry, letters, and mementos? For the incorrigibly nosy, the conscience-challenged, or those women who just have to know, his bathroom can be a goldmine of pertinent information. Are there tampons under his sink? Does he dye his hair, have athlete's foot, or keep a well-stocked porn collection? (Caution: while you're probably safe in your bathroom scrounging, don't even think of pushing that little blinking red light on Mr. Never Worn's cell phone or answering machine—even if he's been evasive about weekend plans or you just *know* there are other females lurking (and there are!). Confirmed bachelors are so territorial about their electronic communication devices that they might as well lift their leg upon said devices to mark them. They hold the evidence of his juggled, often overlapping, relationships. So stay away from his gadgets!

Instead I suggest you gather your information in more forthright ways. For instance, his reputation is a dead giveaway. Talk to other people—especially other women—who know or have known him. Men who avoid intimacy tend to have two different selves. One is a false Self (the one with his group of friends, who think he is nothing less than amazing), and the other is his true Self (the one with the women who will warn you that he is serious bad news). If you find yourself with a man whose dating history could be called *The Neverending Story* or *Around the World in 80 Days*, tell him to hit the road.

8. Faded

Alcoholics, addicts, and guys with addictive personalities all belong in this category, and find themselves at number eight on the toss list. If years of AA meetings or rehab stints interest you, look no further than the Mr. Faded. Unfortunately, just being a male increases your man's risk of addiction. Risk-takers and novelty-seekers who like adrenaline-charged jobs are at even higher risk. These men get bored easily and become hooked on other rushes in order to find excitement. The need for a man to be constantly occupied is an indicator of an addictive personality. When an addicted man accommodates his habits, he thinks he's being productive. He believes that bar-hopping and smoke breaks are vital for his networking. If a Friday night with nothing to do frustrates him, he'll be more likely to find something to do that's addictive.

The inability to tolerate stress is largely why men (or anyone, for that matter) become addicted to substances or behaviors. If you feel powerless in your work or relationship(s), addiction is a way to feel as though you are in control. Social bar-hoppers and workaholics are at risk, but the most likely addicts are men who worry excessively. Low levels of serotonin—the feel-good brain chemical—also appears to be an important cause of addiction. Comfort drugs such as alcohol temporarily increase serotonin levels, as does nicotine. Compulsive gambling is also associated with low levels of serotonin. If a guy doesn't know about or use healthy outlets for stress, then gambling, drinking, smoking, and overeating will always be available to provide their security blankets.

The more easygoing and communicative your man is, the less his chance of becoming an addict. Marriage and committed relationships also appear to provide some protection from addiction problems. Bachelorhood, broken relationships, and divorce are all associated with increased alcohol consumption, whereas marriage is associated with a drop in alcohol consumption.

Whether or not there is truly such a thing as an addictive personality, it is difficult to know which came first—the addiction or the personality disorder. Disorders of stress and anxiety, passive-aggressive tendencies, and antisocial personality disorder are the main culprits of addiction. Unless you are Mother Teresa or Dr. Phil, toss Mr. Faded in the discard pile.

9. Missing a Button

Psychotic and downright dangerous guys belong in this category, and find themselves at number nine on the toss list. If your guy believes much of what his contact on Alpha Centauri tells him, you might consider the possibility that he is one shuttle trip short of the mother ship. This one should be self-explanatory, but we women, being the rescuing and nurturing creatures that we are, may need a reality check. Sometimes, to our own detriment, we hook up with a really troubled or hopelessly ill man. We know to avoid guys who appear insane or abusive; however, some men are quite good at hiding their abnormalities. Although some claim that insanity is a relative term, there are some definitive red flags for us to be aware of. These include: a previous history of mental illness; an addiction to drugs or alcohol; aggression; emotional instability; sharp variations of high energy followed by low energy with depression; suspicious moods; thoughts of conspiracy; insinuations or threats of suicide; hallucinations; and delusions.

Contrary to popular opinion, insanity doesn't have a certain "look" to it; there are perfectly sane men who do howl at the moon and hold meaningful conversations with their houseplants. However, the majority of unusual or bizarre behavior is a red flag to avoid a guy. A guy with one or more of the following symptoms should, without a doubt, be scratched off and banned from your potential partners list:

- Marked personality change.
- Inability to cope with problems and daily activities.
- Strange or grandiose ideas.
- Excessive anxieties.
- Prolonged depression and apathy.
- Marked changes in eating or sleeping patterns.
- Extreme highs and lows.
- Excessive anger, hostility, or violent behavior.
- Overwhelmed by feelings, unable to cope.
- Cries a lot.
- Preoccupied, worried, anxious, and intense.
- Unreasonable fears or phobias.
- Inability to concentrate and a loss of interest in friends.

- Isolates self from other people
- Talks about death or dying
- Has low self-esteem and little self-confidence
- Inability to sleep, sleeping too much, frequent nightmares, or night terrors

10. Stretched Out

Men with heavy debt, who are financially encumbered or bankrupt, extravagant spenders, speculators, and problem and compulsive gamblers all belong in this category, and find themselves at number 10 on the toss list. Admittedly not many of us are putting aside savings to the extent that we should, but the results of hooking up with a man with significant debt can have a far-reaching impact on the quality of your life.

William the Squanderer may have a sob story that he is struggling to repay a school loan; or, he may just be borrowing and charging his way to the American dream. There is some legitimacy that with the increasing cost of living, 20- and 30-somethings are having trouble getting ahead, but it is no justification for bad habits. Gambling, out-of-control cell phone bills, and a life of excess can strap even a generous salary. The result is a no-win scenario of numerous credit cards to fill in financial gaps, and life-ruinous debt.

You are not his mother, teacher, or financial councilor.

There are some substantial differences in the way men and women handle their finances. Women tend to have more credit cards than men, and more credit cards means more debt. Women also use their credit cards for purchases or to pay bills. According to financial experts, they are less likely than men to pay balances on time or pay in full. *Don't* bail him out—you are asking for big trouble. If he is the kind of man you would care to partner with he will dig himself out. If not, then he hasn't matured enough yet to even consider a serious relationship.

What he spends his paycheck on is really none of your business, but if he asks you to borrow money it's time to worry. Men who get themselves heavily encumbered financially are still in short-term mode when it comes to overall lifestyle and mind-set. Although the roving minstrel waxing bohemian can be sexy, bankrolling him for the next 10 years isn't. If you two end up living together, you will need to know that he is stable enough to carry his weight financially. A responsible man who doesn't require immediate gratification is best suited for long-term bonding.

If financial irresponsibility is a pattern for him and he's always in the red, you will be wasting your precious time (and money) if you are looking for a whole and healthy partnership. Be self-aware and keep a separation between your heart and your head. Rid your life of financial parasites and broke, destitute, or bankrupt men. If you are to have any future with William the Squanderer, back off and let him get his financial battlefield in order.

The 8 Male Archetypes: Explore His Sexual Style

16

Read through the following descriptions and discover whether your man is a Wise Guy, Pure Heart, Sultan, Don Juan, Wizard, Mystic, Prince, or Bohemian.

Is He an Enchanting but Unbearable Wise Guy (Pompeius assius)?

"Me, myself, and I" are this boastful buffoon's favorite words. Whatever it is, he's either done it or is an expert at it. The wise guy has a comeback for everything, and can be about as charming as his football buddy's Cheese Whiz and crackers all over your couch. His is a case of "when he is good he is very, very good, but when he is bad, he is horrid." The Wise Guy is reminiscent of the riverboat gambler, the ladies man, and the con man. This classic smartass has a mouth that is only surpassed by his nerve. Appearance-conscious to the point of vanity, the Wise Guy will inevitably steer every conversation back to himself—dysfunctional at best, narcissistic at worst. You hesitate to call it a relationship, as you are the only one actually participating. That's the *Pompeius assius*, our Wise Guy.

Traits of the Wise Guy

- Self-centered.
- Believes that he is unique or special.
- Suffers from approach-retreat romance syndrome.
- Opportunistic and sometimes predatory.
- Capricious, arbitrary, and judgmental.
- Lacks empathy.
- Picky—has a strict checklist of certain qualities he requires in a woman.
- Elusive, detached.

The Wise Guy's sexual style

- Promiscuous.
- Partners tend to be interchangeable.
- Single.
- Exploitive.
- Loves 'em and leaves 'em—one-night stands.
- Suggested Kama Sutra position: the Bee.

Lessons he can teach

- Self-promotion.
- Confidence, action, and skill.

Lessons he needs to learn

- Authenticity.
- Trust.

Turn-ons

- Fellatio.
- Sex with two women.

Is He an Innocent, Playful, Fun-Loving Pure Heart (*Primus puritus*)?

Is your guy a babe in arms? A guiltless, boyish type who is inexperienced and naive in the ways of the world, but ever so anxious for you to teach him? The Pure Heart makes love as if it were his first time. For this relaxed, no-pressure kind of a guy, the feelings involved are as important as the sexual act itself. If you are with this sweet, attentive, and patient guy, welcome to sex on the Planet of Yes. This playful and loving guy trusts with no agendas. He is tuned into his senses but is not primarily focused on his genitals. His upbeat and optimistic attitude gives him a healthy sexual appetite, sans the kink. He finds a white cotton chemise or your innocent babydolls sexier than a black lace teddy any day. In addition, he really does think you are beautiful without makeup. In fact, he thinks you look perfect. That's *Primus puritus*, our Pure Heart.

Traits of the Pure Heart

- Sincere.
- Inexperienced.
- Law abiding.
- Longsuffering.
- Loyal.
- Gentle.

- Committed.
- Involved.

The Pure Heart's sexual style

- Caressing, kissing, and no goals of orgasm.
- Makes an emotional connection with his lover.
- Likes the preliminaries in love (foreplay).
- Simple—asks, "Can I kiss you?"
- Connected, playful, vulnerable sex.
- Suggested Kama Sutra positions: classic missionary, Lotus.

Lessons he can teach

- Unconditional love.
- Trust.
- Simplicity.

Lessons he needs to learn

- Self-confidence.
- Assertiveness, how to take control or make decisions.

Turn-ons

- Long talks.
- Holding hands.
- Face-to-face contact.

- Intimate sex.
- Safety.
- Trust.

Is He an Adventurous, Exploratory, and Daring Sultan (*Spurius sultanicus*)?

Like a camel that can go for long periods of time without water, the Sultan can go for long periods of time without a relationship, waiting for his ideal woman. It is quality, not quantity, that he desires, and his patience is as vast as the sands. If he chooses you, it's because he really wants to be with you, not because he just needs to be with someone. He is thrilled to be in a relationship, but only as long as *you* cater to his every whim. The problem with Sultan types is that this isn't the 13th century. The women's liberation movement pretty much took the buzz off the whole "women as chattel" thing. He keeps getting older, but the women he dates do not. That's our *Spurius sultanicus*, the Sultan.

Traits of the Sultan

- Possessive.
- Suffocating—you belong to him entirely.
- Chauvinistic.

- Demanding.
- Picky.
- Blessed by birth.
- Entitled.
- Harsh.
- In control.

The Sultan's sexual style

- Mature, slow hand.
- Experienced.
- Male superior, female submissive.
- Suggested Kama Sutra position: the Stag.

Lessons he can teach

- Traditional male/female relationship.
- Patience.
- High standards of quality and beauty.

Lessons he needs to learn

- Equality with women.
- More about his yin nature/feminine side.

Turn-ons

- Younger women.
- Male superior, rear entry.

- Fellatio.
- Traditional missionary position.

Is He a Sensual, Passionate, Hot-Blooded Don Juan (*Philanderus don juanicus*)?

The legendary Spanish noblemen had nothing on this paramour. A charming womanizer, heartbreaker, ladies man, and all-around philanderer, this bad boy of the bedroom and swashbuckler of the sheets is part pirate, part conqueror. His kind of sex is heart-pumping, and he enjoys pushing past comfort zones. Dramatic tension is the mood, and if it challenges sexual boundaries, count him in. This open-minded adventurer views the dating world as his own personal smorgasbord. He's with a hot New York model one week and a successful career woman the next. A particular favorite of his is married women, as they rarely ask him to make a commitment. Our *Philanderus don juanicus* likes to keep his options open.

Traits of the Don Juan

- Super-attentive, with a seemingly intense interest in you.
- The less interested you seem, the more ardently he pursues.

- Commitment phobic—don't hold your breath waiting for him to settle down.
- Flowery e-mails, frequent phone calls, fabulous first dates.
- Once you're hooked, he wants out—the fun is in the chase.
- Will "hump and dump"—sexually exploitive.
- Many sexual partners (polyamorous).
- Single or never married.

The Don Juan's sexual style

- Approach-avoidance cycle—he's a tease.
- Pushes the envelope with risky or even dangerous sex.
- Experimental, bold, unconventional.
- Lustful.
- Prefers short-term relationships.
- Suggested Kama Sutra positions: the Crow, the Bamboo.

Lessons he can teach

- Pushing past fear.
- Detachment.
- Adventure.

Lessons he has to learn

- Bonding.
- Internal rather than external power.

Turn-ons

- Vulnerable women.
- Outrageous, fetish sex.
- Group sex.

Is He an Earthy, Wiccan Wizard (Sextus magicus)?

High on ego and low on conventionality, the Wizard is a transformer of women's desires. He has his roots deep in the earthly elements. Astute in the art of pleasure, expanded consciousness is his aim and transfixing women is his game. He cooks, gardens organically, and grows his own medicinal herbs. The Wizard is a psychic cross between Dr. Timothy Leary and Criss Angel.

Our Wizard differs from Don Juan in the depths of his emotional investment. Both are wary of marriage and commitment, but Don Juan has bonding issues, whereas the Wizard is merely a solitary man with a lone wolf destiny. Romantically, the wizard can be an elusive, even frustrating, lover, giving just enough of his time and energy to keep you interested. This is a man who will always need his personal freedom. He may vanish as quickly as he arrived, but not without casting some memorable spells on your heart. That's *Sextus magicus*, our Wizard.

Traits of the Wizard

- Unpredictable.
- Intense.
- Prefers admiration over love.
- Sexual apprenticeship—he's the teacher, you're the student.
- Skillful in new or novel sexual techniques and positions.
- Intuitive, shaman, healer, and dreamer of dreams.
- Likely to explore alternative sexuality in some form.
- Picky—has strict checklist of certain qualities he requires in a woman.
- Elusive, detached.

The Wizard's sexual style

- Intense.
- Transformative.
- Experimental.
- Skilled in tantric and Taoist sexual techniques.
- Eclectic.
- Suggested Kama Sutra positions: the Yawning, the Lotus.

Lessons he can teach

- Sex as a ceremony.
- Experiencing the spiritual through the physical.
- The importance of the mind in sexuality.

Lessons he has to learn

- Humility.
- Attachment.

Turn-ons

- Kinky sex.
- Mind-expanding substances.
- Power exchange.

Is He an Obscure, Otherworldly Mystic (*Marcus mysticus*)?

Does your guy see hidden meaning in everything? The mystic always has to clarify which life he is talking about. He makes love to the cosmos as well as you, and his lovemaking is a melding of body, soul, and spirit. An esoteric experience awaits this gentleman's bed partner. Metaphysical shaman extraordinaire, you could find him at a metaphysical retreat or celebrating the Solstice at Stonehenge. He holds mystical views about sex; you belong to him by way of secret rites, and once initiated, your sex life sizzles! Sex with the Mystic is

to join yin and yang in universal unity. Waves of bliss await you in your own sacred love temple with *Marcus mysticus*, our Mystic.

Traits of the Mystic

- Uninhibited.
- Otherworldly.
- Intuitive.
- Spiritual.
- Emotional.
- Enjoys altered states of consciousness.
- Aroused by beauty.
- Looks for the cause in the effect.

The Mystic's sexual style

- Wants to merge with his partner.
- Sexual experience akin to a religious experience.
- Cosmic intercourse.
- Makes love to reconnect with the universe.
- Endless pleasure.
- Suggested Kama Sutra positions: the Conch, the Lotus.

Lessons he can teach

- Spiritual enlightenment through sexual activity.
- Being in touch with the cosmos.
- Detachment.

Lessons he must learn

- How to live in the here and now.
- Attachment.

Turn-ons

- Candles, incense, music.
- Eye-to-eye sex.
- Sex on a mountaintop.

Is He a Nurturing, Caretaking Prince (*Servius maximus*)?

His forte is taking care of you—body, mind, and soul. Cuddling and snuggling awaits his beloved as does breakfast in bed and foot massages. He buffers you from harsh reality and you both like it that way. This is a guy who aims to please his lady. Service, investment, and involvement define his romantic interactions.

The Prince will help you put on your pajamas and lovingly rub your aching back. He'll tuck the covers up over your shoulders with almost parental devotion. You can feel his love. He prefers sex that is comfortable, familiar, and intimate. Matters of the heart are always serious business to this romantic. Because he's turned off by the bar scene, you'll find him settling in for a long evening with his soul mate. He is in the game of love for keeps. That's *Servius maximus*, our Prince.

Traits of the Prince

- Affectionate.
- Homey.
- Comfortable.
- Appreciative.
- Generous.
- Caters to partner—lets the woman make decisions.
- Doesn't exhibit alpha male behavior, even in a group.

The Prince's sexual style

- To become one with his partner.
- Sex represents commitment to him.
- Has endurance—a marathon man in the bedroom.
- A slow hand and attention to foreplay.
- Eye-to-eye intercourse.
- Suggested Kama Sutra positions: the Elephant, the Bee.

Lessons he can teach

- Unconditional love.
- Service.
- Gaining pleasure through giving.

Lessons he needs to learn

- Releasing insecurity.
- Self-confidence.

Turn-ons

- Making love with a soul mate.
- Romance, ambiance.
- Slow seduction.

Is He an Artistic, Creative Bohemian (*Musicus opius*)?

Writer of love poems, plays, and operas, this true sexual maestro plays his lover like a fine violin. You may find yourself posing for his next oil painting or inspiring his next symphony. A true Renaissance man, his presence in your life bodes well for you, for you are his love, his heart, and his passion.

This restless vagabond of the bedroom is an artistic adventurer who possesses free morals, unconventional habits, and some interesting sexual tastes. You're the best of friends. You cook dinners together, rent movies, crash in each other's apartments, and, for all intents and purposes, act like a couple. But if you want to take the relationship further, he asserts that your "outstanding friendship" is satisfying enough. He gets an ego boost from knowing you want him, knowing full well that you don't have a chance to keep him. That's *Musicus opius*, our Bohemian.

Traits of the Bohemian

- Gifted in the fine arts and literature.
- Fun to be with—friendly, sociable, and a great storyteller.
- Commitment phobic.
- Lacks ambition in the material sense.
- Capricious, changeable.
- Passes the buck, resists responsibility for outcomes.
- Chooses partners from large pool of friends.

The Bohemian's sexual style

- Fantasy prone.
- Makes love "next to" his partner rather than "with" her.
- Unconventional sex such as threesomes and group sex.

- Promiscuous—usually has another woman lined up in the wings.
- Suggested Kama Sutra positions: the Crow, the Lotus, the Bee.

Lessons he can teach

- Spontaneity.
- Variety.
- Unfettered creativity.

Lessons he has to learn

- Exclusivity.
- Intimacy.

Turn-ons

- Freedom.
- Beauty.
- Creativity.

Do's and Don'ts of Dating: Some Words of Wisdom

17

The golden rule of dating is to be courteous, listen, and ask questions. If you want to be thought of as a great date, learn to listen to what he says, ask questions, and then ask more questions! Few things are as damaging to relationships as selfishness. It is impossible to be in tune with another person when you are self-absorbed and easily distracted by how everything relates to you personally. The old comedy line, "Well, that's enough about me, let's talk about me for a while," is humorous, but it's also a big red flag. Thinking that love is in short supply is neither correct nor healthy. You have many soul mates and spiritual partners who will come into your life at appointed times. You need only be receptive. "There's a trolley by every 20 minutes," as my great-aunt would say.

Dating Checklist

- Always try to bring good energy and attitude to your dates.

- Relax and have fun. This shouldn't feel like an interrogation or job interview.

- Point out your date's positive attributes (even the coolest cat likes to hear praise).

- If you are not interested in seeing him again, just tell him as gently as possible. Insinuating something while meaning something else can result in a painful sting to the one being deceived.

- Date people who have similar values to your own. Major categories of contention are religion, politics, and sex.

- Don't call someone more than once a day, unless they reply. (Desperation is a huge turnoff.)

- Don't repeat the mistakes of the past and continually date the same kinds of love loonies.

- ∞ Don't lie to your date or pretend to be something you're not. If things work out, having to confess a lie down the way could be disastrous!
- ∞ Don't tell everything about yourself from the start. Keep a little mystery, and he'll be left wanting to know more.
- ∞ Don't get drunk on a date! Need I elaborate on this one? You'll end up being one of Snow White's seven drunken bimbos: Tipsy, Woozy, Dizzy, Pukey, Horny, Bitchy, or Needy.
- ∞ Don't date a married person! If they have good intentions they will leave their partner before pursuing another person. If you are married, separate first. If you are single, you deserve better.

Some Words of Wisdom

Get your own act together first

The Chinese sage Lao Tze once said: "He who knows others is learned; he who knows himself is wise." Knowing who you are and what you want out of life is the cornerstone of any relationship of substance. No person can make you feel better about yourself; that can only be generated internally.

Stop choosing dysfunctional men

If it looks like a tree, smells like a tree, and acts like a tree, consider that it might be a tree! Some women choose the same type of troubled partners again and again. Can you really claim to be surprised when these same patterns repeat if you keep choosing damaged men? Stop the cycle by being aware.

Be yourself

According to the true law of attraction, real attracts real. Without the ability to be authentic there can be no real connection. Twisting yourself into a pretzel to please a man is a sure way to alienate him, and a sure way to make you neurotic. Don't pretend to be something you're not, and try to be interested only in those men who are quite obviously interested in you.

Don't adjust my knobs; they are perfectly tuned

Saying "I will redo" instead of "I do" is a lesson in futility. Trying to change or fix the other person by changing yourself or through manipulation can be disastrous. It's neither your job nor your right to judge or change a man. Know who you are and then get to know who he really is. Use your whole being to discern if someone is right for you.

5 Steps on the Stairway to Relationship Heaven

1. Be clear. Although some partners may be psychic, most are not. Being straightforward with your wants and needs is critical for a successful relationship. Trying to second-guess your partner or playing the guess-why-I'm-upset game inevitably invites communication problems and misunderstandings. Giving your partner the silent treatment is not only childish; it is a devastating blow to intimacy.

2. Be affectionate. We are sensory creatures. We communicate in a special way by means of touch. Endorphins, dopamine, and other "feel-good" neurotransmitters fire off their magic when we are touched, hugged, or caressed. Physical expressions of love and affection allow a special kind of closeness between a couple. A lack of it creates separation and distance.

3. Be spiritual. With the presence of a higher being or Creator in our lives, we will naturally elevate our relationships to a higher plane. Awareness of karma has an amazing way of enhancing a relationship. Caring, kindness, and forgiveness naturally follow the awareness of

spiritual responsibility. Your partnership cannot grow until you acknowledge that a higher purpose is guiding the relationship.

4. Be friends. Friendship is the glue that holds long-term relationships together. Your lover must also be your best friend, your confidant, your biggest fan, and your general partner in crime. A strong friendship is the best way to defend your relationship against third parties, sick children, annoying relatives, negative neighbors, and impossible bosses.

5. Know the laws of the jungle. On a first or second date you can already tell if he is trouble. Does he tend to blame the waitress, the weather, the government, fate, or even you for his his own mistakes, mishaps, predicaments, and failures? Is he hypersensitive? Is he easily slighted, injured, or insulted? Does he treat animals and children impatiently or cruelly? Is he hostile or disdainful toward the weak, the poor, or the disabled? Does he confess to having a difficult history with women? Is he too eager? Does he want to move in together after having dated you only twice? Does he act jealous when you talk to other men? Does he disrespect your boundaries or treat you as an object? Does he disapprove if you are away for too long, and does he interrogate you when

you return? Does he emphasize your most minute faults (devalue you), or does he exaggerate your talents, traits, and skills (idealize you)? Does he find sadistic sex exciting? Is he too forceful with you or does he enjoy hurting you physically? If you have answered yes to any of the above, run for the hills and stay away. He's trouble!

The Secret Signals of Dysfunctional Men

Some bad men are an elusive breed—difficult to spot and even more difficult to pin down. However, even these men send out subtle, almost subliminal, signals:

- Haughty body language—a posture or facial expression of superiority, seniority, hidden powers, mysteriousness, and/or amused indifference.
- Entitlement—he expects special treatment.
- Idealization or devaluation of others.
- The ambivalent "membership" posture—he instantly tries to belong yet keeps his distance.

These guys fancy themselves as Renaissance men, yet they are merely fearful little boys turned predators—the proverbial wolves in sheep's clothing.

Bad Boys: Players, Perverts, and Master Sinisters

18

I refuse to belong to any club that will accept me as a member.

—Groucho Marx

Whether rebel, gigolo, or full-fledged "master sinister," since time immemorial, bad boys have held a particular fascination for women. We love them when they take us to the top of love's mountain, and scorn them when they leave us face down in its valleys. Anyone who's been in the dating world longer than 10 minutes knows the highs and lows of such relationships.

The bad boy's excessive self-confidence—or more precisely, his arrogance—and his unpredictable, "misunderstood" nature is what attracts us to him in the first place. We tend to think of bad boys as naughty little creatures who just can't help themselves. They are very sexy and usually great in bed. Many girls go after bad boys for their excitement potential; others do it for the challenge. With our female egos we think, "With my unique charms I'll be the one to finally settle this wild man down." However, this is a man who manipulates a woman's feelings. Using mega charm and his streetwise cool, the bad boy has his act down pat. He cruises like a shark hunting for women with low self-esteem.

These philanderers and schemers are used to getting their way. When they don't they simply move on. A bad boy will seldom feel guilty for hurting your feelings, and will dash off to his next interest faster than you can say "hump and dump." Bad boys seek to notch their belts with as many sexual conquests as possible. Sometimes we choose this type of guy over and over again. Oftentimes we know going into the relationship that this man is problematic, yet we always act surprised when he breaks our heart.

Just in case your relationship radar needs a little fine tuning, here are some signs that you might be involved with a bad boy:

 ∞ He views dating as a numbers game and tries to meet as many women as possible.

- He recycles (revisits) old flames during "slump" periods. This is a biggie—some bad boys have kept women strung along for years.

- He has short-term relationships for weeks or months, not years.

- He won't commit; he'll keep his options open just in case someone better comes along.

- He scopes out every female he sees, mentally mapping out his next date. He boorishly flirts with waitresses and brags about his past sexual conquests.

- He knows how to rise (ahem) to the occasion in the bedroom. The problem is that he does it so frequently with other women. This guy is not yours alone.

- He isn't interested in hanging around after sex and will predictably bail before brunch.

Bad boys play upon the certainty that women want to feel that they are different than all the other girls, but the truth is that he has no intention of settling down with you or anyone else. So when all is said and done, are bad boys worth the ride? Read on.

Gigolos and Con Men

A gigolo is a Casanova of a gent whose main income is derived from gifts or payments from women in return for his sexual favors or companionship. Never succumb to the temptation to invest your time, heart, or money on this smooth seducer. What a gigolo offers a successful woman is, plain and simple, an atrocious business deal. Here's why: A relationship with Giovanni Gigolo is a trade. He brings his looks and bedroom talents, and you bring your money. If you finance his next "project," he'll call you, hang out with you, and have sex with you. But here's the rub: His looks, health, charm, and erections will fade, but your income will most likely continue to increase. In economic terms, he is a depreciating asset and you are an appreciating, or earning, asset. On Wall Street, Giovanni Gigolo would be considered a "trade," not a "buy and hold." The "efficient market" concept would contend that something is wrong with him: Ask yourself why such a catch would not be married or otherwise taken?

Confidence men, or con men, are the narcissistic sociopaths of the dating world. While the bad boys and gigolos actively search for certain women, the con man is much more diabolical. The con man is the bad boy on steroids—a swindler who exploits women by means of deception or fraud. Confidence and independence are very attractive traits in a man, and women looking for a strong partner are the ones who are most frequently caught in his trap. This predator knows that timing is everything, and uses an air of mystery to his advantage.

Con men know women. They use tactics such as love poems, romantic environments, and bogus stories of danger and bravery to captivate women. Pathological liar extraordinaire, the con man will claim that he had a promising career, brilliant future, and large trust fund, all of which were snatched away from him due to some unfair turn of events or accident. He needs your sympathy—and your money. It is easy to believe that he really loves you. However, if and when the money runs dry, he'll just move on to find a new partner/victim.

Confidence men are the worst of the worst. They look for vulnerable women, widows, newly divorced women, spinsters, and women recovering from heartbreak. These lotharios lurk as they look forward to financial pillage. They will romance you and then say something such as, "I love you too much to take you away from your friends and family, but I'll always be close by." Once he is involved in your life and in your finances, you will have a real job getting him out again.

The "Master Sinister"—the World of BDSM

When I began this book by asserting that every dotless set of dice and depraved degenerate found me absolutely irresistible, maybe you thought I was kidding. Sexually, I am what's called a "vanilla." That's a feeble epithet for all things simple, plain, and ordinary—that is, boring—sexually speaking. I've noticed that it's cool to be kinky. Truthfully I wish I were more perverted, but I don't seem to "get" that particular leaning.

The term BDSM is an abbreviation derived from bondage and discipline, domination and submission, and sadism and masochism. "All that exists is you and me and the sound of my voice," whispers the costume-clad dominatrix to her bound and gagged "submissive." This isn't dialog from a bad B movie; it's part of the lifestyle of a surprising number of men and women. Call me silly, but putting on a leather harness, 6-inch-high stilettos, and cracking a whip makes me want to go trick-or-treating—not have an orgasm.

BDSM, or fetish role playing, is an exchange of power between two people; one assumes the dominant master or mistress role, and the other becomes his or her submissive, or "bottom." Generally speaking, men who are into this type of sexual expression usually have issues with both control and trust—two minefield areas in relationships. If your guy is into vampires or the Goth scene, or thinks Vlad the Impaler was a pretty cool dude, you'll want to read on.

When Donny Dungeonmaster looks at you, smiles lustily, and whispers, "Nice spankable butt, baby," you blush and flush and your brain floods with endorphins. Your excitement builds for this "master sinister" who wants to introduce you to some forbidden fruits. *What's the harm*, you ask your-self. *Heck, I'm adventurous, and even a little curious.* Whoa there, sister! Whether online or in real life, the odds are fairly high that at some time in your dating life, you will meet a Donny Dungeonmaster who wants to introduce you to the world of rough sex. Within the vast ocean of human sexual preferences, there are a few "rogue waves" that stand out due to their potential for danger, their delusional quality, or the sheer gross-out factor involved. The convoluted world of BDSM is one of these.

So, what if Mr. Dungeonmaster wants to give you a few playful smacks on the bottom? In the interest of fairness, I will try to let you form your own opinion. I asked an ac-quaintance of mine (the oh-so-edgy "Lady Badger") why a woman would be into the BDSM scene. You guessed it—it's a "spiritual thing" (and I was thinking it was merely simple assault). I realized then that people who are into this lifestyle have elevated their perversity to a spiritual experience. Nirvana, she claimed, is something called "subspace" or "domspace"— numb states in which the endorphins that have been released to combat pain have buzzed the senses. But as we know, pain is your body's way of telling you that something is wrong. Sadomasochism may not be morally wrong or evil, but from your body's point of view, it is definitely a stupid thing to do.

Consider some of the alarming book titles available within the S and M subculture. You can read such literary greats as *The Joys of Servitude to Big Daddy Mo* by slavebecky (one word, lower case), or *Electrical Play and Erotic Nipple Torture for Beginners* by Master Dom Sir. Or perhaps *Decorative Rope Bondage* by Mistress Cuckold is more up your alley. (By decorative I am assuming it's important to look your best while you're bound and gagged.) Most titles are distasteful yet humorous, whereas others, such as *Medical Probes and Catheters* by Nurse Pester, are downright scary and dangerous.

As I mentioned earlier, "vanilla" is used in a condescending way by those into S and M to describe boring, conventional sex. Speaking of flavors, here's a partial list of the not so delicious tastes offered at your average play party or dungeon social. As you will see, you won't need nuts on any of these flavors—there are plenty already! Classes include: Rope Bondage, Whipping, Spanking, Slave Training, Knife Play, Humiliation and Interrogation, Electrical Play, Feminization, English Caning, Domestic Discipline, Nipple Torture, Flogging, Breath Play, Body Punching and Slapping, Fire Play, Singletail Whips, Hot Wax, Mummification, Sounds and Urethral Play, Suspension and Flesh Hooks, and Terror Play. *Terror Play?* How's that one for a jaw dropper? Apparently it's a turn-on for some people to recreate the same mental trauma and panic that formed their warped sexuality in the first place.

Ah, the cornerstones of any successful relationship!

And, if that's not enough to make you want to give up sex altogether, how about the BDSM practice of branding (yes, as in cows). Now there's a sexy evening—the lights are low, love talk is whispered, so what better time to whip out the family branding iron? Just coo, "Honey, can you heat up the coals?" My personal favorite stomach-turner is something called a "collaring ceremony." Those into BDSM don't indulge in the antiquated institution of marriage. The master, or dominant, actually puts a collar onto his slave or submissive. In the BDSM lifestyle, one becomes "collared," not married. (I know—I'll never buy another choker necklace again, either.)

I may be missing something here, but how "spiritual" can these sexual activities be? Let's go back to the initial question. What if Donny Dungeonmaster wants to give you a few playful swats on the fanny? Consider that men who prefer to express their sexuality in such ways may have issues. Granted, we all have issues, but most women are utterly unprepared to encounter these particular perversions. With the increasing acceptance of this lifestyle, the odds are high that you, too, will someday encounter your own Donny D. Never is the "eyes-wide-open" (EWO) principle more critical than when exploring the world of alternative sexuality.

Heaven help Vickie Vanilla who falls in love with Perverted Pete. Vickie, whose idea of pleasure is a warm bath and a back rub, finds herself tolerating Pete's unappealing kinks with the kind of maternal devotion seen in primate documentaries. What is really going on here? The submissives, or "subs," are fearful, covert pleasers who use the structured world of BDSM as a cloak for insecurity and neediness. The dominants, or "doms," are fearful, seething pots of anger who use the structured world of BDSM as an outlet for sadistic urges and pent up rage. Both are manipulative, both are fearful, and both are using the other to numb painful feelings. These two are just part of the lunatic fringe who identify themselves primarily by their sexual orientation. Many live marginal lives in other areas and suffer from some cataclysmic personality disorders.

So, what does it take to leap from a boring, "vanilla" sex life to this enlightened version of the medieval barber surgeon? Behaviorists have traditionally said that trauma is the cause. However, because the psychiatric DSM IV-TR of mental illnesses has reclassified sadism and masochism as paraphilias, BDSM is considered abnormal only if it causes "significant distress" to the individual. If you're fine with it, it's all good. And why shy away from such proclivities when you can get together with other like-minded cohorts and rationalize that this is a normal and even superior expression of sexuality? The "munch" is one of the ways BDSM practitioners get together to do this. Munches are luncheons held in public places where BDSM-ers meet and chime in on such topic gems as what makes a single-tail whip crack, or what they are looking for in a dominant/slave relationship.

Again, the likelihood of your dating or meeting someone at some point in your life who is into this lifestyle is high.

While still regarded as a subculture within mainstream society, the BDSM community exists in large cities and small towns alike. Just in case you are ever curious or tempted to succumb to the lure of the ultimate bad boy, here's your EWO reality check, the ultimate look before you leap. What are the unseen spiritual dynamics occurring here? What predisposes someone to prefer or even require the power-play of sadomasochism over the kinder, gentler forms of love? *Pain to initiate pleasure and violence to express love indicates a conflict between the personality and the soul.* In this scenario, the body, mind, and spirit are incommunicado. The truth is that sadomasochism is not a higher level on the sexual evolutionary plane; it is more in line with a primitive past, when the pursuit of external power, rather than internal power, was the name of the game.

I would submit that all perversions are sexual manifestations of structural defects. In plain talk this means that Donny Dungeonmaster's disturbed sex life is only the tip of the iceberg in his cockeyed personality. Dominance and submission both originate from the same source—fear of painful emotions. The "props" of BDSM—the drama, the masks, the scenes—cover up and encase painful feelings with painful sensations. Both doms and subs have issues with authority in some way. Both dominants and submissives are simmering volcanoes of pain waiting to erupt. The need to dominate is an expression of fear, pain, and anger, and the need to submit is a frightened expression of a need to please. Both souls are terrified and feel unworthy. The exchange of power that occurs within BDSM circles is nothing more than an attempt to obtain power externally. The dominant sadist controls overtly, and the submissive masochist manipulates covertly. Physiologically, when pain and powerlessness are combined with the libido, the regions of the brain that manage sexual stimuli become intertwined with those that manage pain.

So what does karma have to do with BDSM? Sexuality is a common arena in which psychic dramas are played out in full view. The human personality is desperately seeking its soul component. In someone with sadomasochistic tendencies, communication between the soul and the personality may have been disconnected by early conditioning. The pain of BDSM is a distraction for the personality and the senses, while the soul tries to reintegrate them back together as one. Should you stay with, or even consider a relationship with, someone like this? The Marquis de Sade is probably not the package that an enlightened man is going to come wrapped in. Those who practice BDSM desire to be free of any responsibility—even if it's to their own sexuality.

Part III
Kama: Erotic and Sexual Pleasure

Seduction, Atmosphere, and Romance

19

An ideal way to set the stage for satisfying seduction and remarkable romance is to nurture the senses with tantalizing scents, soothing ambiance, and relaxing music. Harmonize your love nest with subtle lighting, beautiful objects, and erotic scents to stimulate your romantic mind.

Erotic sights, smells, and sounds increase brain function in the hypothalamus and the occipital and frontal brain lobes, which simultaneously decreases activity in both temporal lobes of the brain. This decreased activity in the temporal lobes deactivates inhibition, embarrassment, and moral judgment during sexual arousal. In contrast, when we are stressed, frightened, or angry, the "fight-or-flight" hormones, such as adrenaline, are released, which blocks activation of the arousal areas of the brain and activates the temporal lobe areas responsible for apprehension. This causes inhibition and a lack of sexual desire. Stress, fear, and anger are the death blows to a good sexual experience. The path to great sex is paved with relaxation.

Aromatherapy for Lovers

There is a long and rich history of using the olfactory sense to enhance sexuality. Essential oils and scents stimulate the brain's limbic system to relax, to transform spiritually, and to come alive sexually. Essential oils are distilled by steam or water from the various parts of plants. Some of these essential and precious oils come from herbs, roots, and bark, and others are derived from fruits, flowers, and seeds. For centuries they have been used for their meditative, calming, and beneficial properties. Essential oils can be released using an aroma lamp, added to a warm bath, or mixed with a carrier oil for sensual massage.

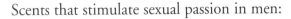

Scents that stimulate sexual passion in men:

- Cinnamon—warm, spicy, aphrodisiacal.
- Sandalwood—sweet, woody, erogenous.
- Musk and balsam—aphrodisiacal, erotic, earthy.
- Cedarwood—harmonious, meditative, woodsy.
- Vanilla—warm, delicious, sensual.
- Patchouli—smoky, earthy, erogenous.

Scents that stimulate romantic passion in women:

- Rose—sweet, promotes romantic love, dispels grief.
- Orange—fruity, harmonizes, brings joy.
- Rosemary—relaxing, sexually arousing.
- Amber—sweet, erogenous, musky.
- Lavender—sweet, relaxing, antidepressant.
- Jasmine—honey-like, powerful aphrodisiac.

Sensual Massage

The skin is the largest organ of the body and home to millions of nerve endings that send sensory messages to the brain. Sensual massage has long been used as a therapeutic tool for health and happiness. It's also a surefire way to get your lover into a romantic mood. Specific massage techniques are not as important as you and your partner just relaxing and enjoying each other. Intimate touch encourages us to open up to our partner, to relax, and to be vulnerable in trust. Massage builds familiarity and is a pleasurable way to enhance intimacy. It is also just the ticket to quickly drop inhibitions and build closeness between lovers.

Sensual massage invites passion and erotic love as well. Practiced in many cultures and lands, it is more than simple rubbing and kneading of muscles. At its best, it can be a total body/mind/soul experience. It is a fusion of atmosphere, spiritual energy, and bodily response. Stress is relieved, frazzled nerves loosen up, and the muscles begin to relax. Sensual massage is erotic in that it arouses all six senses. From raw physical passion to deep spiritual fusion, sensual massage is most rewarding when there is an emotional bond between a couple. It can be an intimate form of communication that eliminates the need for words. This type of physical contact encourages trust and affection, and intensifies sexual response and orgasm. So, whether it's Thai or Swedish massage, Asian acupressure, shiatsu, or therapeutic or erotic massage, learn a few new techniques and have fun!

Aromatherapy mixtures for sensual massage

Select your favorite essential oil and mix it together with 6 ounces of almond, grapeseed, or jojoba oil to create an aromatic sensual massage oil. Mineral or baby oil tends to be too heavy and is best avoided. To make a more concentrated perfume to dab on here and there, decrease oil from 6 ounces

to 1/4 ounce. Use the recipes below, or create your own signature scents.

Try:

- 8 drops of sandalwood
- 4 drops orange
- 2 drops cinnamon
- 2 drops rose

Or:

- 6 drops cinnamon
- 4 drops orange
- 2 drops jasmine

Or:

- 4 drops of sandalwood
- 4 drops rosemary
- 2 drops orange
- 2 drops lavender

For spiritual enlightenment

Amber (styrax) is a pure oil extracted from tree resin. It connects the physical with the spiritual—personality with spirit—and stimulates the seventh chakra located at the crown of your head.

For sexual stimulation

Musk (ambretta) is a legendary aphrodisiac and stimulates the second chakra located in the middle of your lower abdomen. Musk stimulates sexual appetite and vitality.

For love, compassion, and friendship

Rose is what is called a "heart scent," as it awakens the fourth chakra located at the spine behind the heart. Rose promotes love, openness, and friendship.

Colors and Candles

Colors are light radiations from the realm of the spirit. Our responses to colors run deep, as each color of the rainbow allows us a sensory glimpse into the divine. Candles contribute a pleasant ambiance to your cozy casbah and stimulate the Fire element responsible for passion, arousal, and resolution. Each color of the quartz visible light spectrum has its own unique qualities. Choose the mood and type of romance you wish to attract by selecting the corresponding candle color. Combine candles with your choice of aromatic oils, and you set the mood for some seriously entrancing lovemaking!

To attract:

- Gentleness, love, and loyalty—pink candle.
- Romance, strength, and sexual passion—crimson or flame-red candle.

- Longevity, healing, and fertility—forest green candle.
- Alignment, bonding, and soulmating with a partner—dark blue or indigo candle.
- Spiritual awakening, enlightenment—purple or violet candle.
- Safety, protection, and relaxation—light or medium blue candle.
- New starts, beginnings, purity, and mercy—white candle.
- Energy and alertness—orange candle.
- Centering and communication—yellow candle.
- Spiritual attainment—gold candle.

Rock Your Casbah

Prepare your bedroom for passion using sensual textures and inviting fabrics such as silk, satin, velvet, and soft cottons. Decide what effect you are trying to achieve. Is it an understated, restrained, or subtle feel? Or a bold, arousing, dramatic look? Rich colors of emerald green, indigo blue, and fuchsia can transform even the most boring bedroom into a sultry boudoir. Start with silk sheets in gold, top with an embroidered satin comforter in rich jewel tones, and accent with overstuffed velvet pillows. For a truly elegant look, make a simple canopy over your bed by draping your favorite material.

An innocent white cotton and lace motif is also very sexy, and a white gauze mosquito net above the bed makes for a romantic cloud. Whatever style you choose, be sure to add some fresh flowers such as lilies, daisies, freesias, tulips, roses, gardenias, lilacs, or wildflowers.

Kama Sutra Positions for Enchanted Lovers

20

The combining of eroticism with spirituality is almost exclusively an Eastern concept. Both tantra (India) and Taoism (China) are concerned with balancing the masculine and feminine energies. Chinese Taoist practice calls these the yin and yang energies, whereas Indian tantric practice refers to these essential energies as Shakti and Shiva. As pioneers in spiritual sexuality, both Taoist and tantric sexual concepts share a common goal of uniting the physical with the spiritual. Exchanging sexual energy with a partner works best when both people are mentally and spiritually on the same page. The Kama Sutra indulges the five senses of sound, touch, sight, taste, and scent. These, united with our sixth sense of intuition/spirit, are indeed the stairway to heaven.

Sometime between the first and sixth centuries, a Brahmin named Vatsyayana compiled the most extensive collection of social-sexual literature ever assembled, called the Kama Sutra. Loosely translated, Kama Sutra is Sanskrit for "aphorisms of love," with Kama meaning desire and Sutra meaning rules. "Desire" includes the 64 arts from Chapter 10 (singing, reading, poetry, dancing, and so on) in addition to the sexual arts, all of which were illustrated in the ancient pages of this remarkable book. In addition to being an historic as well as cultural document, it is essentially a technical guide to sexual pleasures. By creating this work, Vatsyayana elevated the art of ecstasy to a spiritual experience. This encyclopedic 6th-century formulary introduced the "three aims of life":

1. Dharma—spirituality, virtue, and ethics.

2. Artha—prosperity and material happiness.

3. Kama—erotic and sexual pleasure.

You can see that virtue, prosperity, and eroticism are mutually interdependent. Our conscience needs ethics (dharma), our well-being needs material security (artha), and our body needs sexual satisfaction (kama). The Kama Sutra describes making love as a "divine union." Vatsyayana believed that sex itself was not wrong, but doing it badly was! Here are just a few of the many sexual positions and techniques, in order of popularity. Have fun with these and enjoy some variations of your own. After all, we wouldn't want to do it badly!

Milking

This is a technique that every woman should learn. The art of milking involves using your PC (pubococcygeus) muscle in a rippling motion when squeezing your man's penis. This is the same rippling effect that happens in the vagina during orgasm. The rippling causes a kind of milking action that starts at one end of the vagina and moves along to the other end. Mind-blowing for him to say the least!

The Mare

The trick to this technique is holding your lover's penis tightly inside of you by bringing your legs tightly together while tightening your vaginal muscles. When you become really good at this, in addition to sending your man into nirvana, you can constrict the blood in the penis, thus helping him maintain an erection.

The Bee

In this female-superior position, the man lies down on his back with his legs outstretched. The woman sits on top of him, allowing him to penetrate her. The woman controls the thrusting movements while the man stimulates her clitoris with his hand. This position affords some of the deepest penetration possible. The man has the added pleasure of relaxing and watching his lady on top. As a variation, try leaning back and twisting from side to side. You can rotate your hips so that his penis circles deep within. This Bee is a keeper!

The Elephant

This is a variation on the classic rear-entry position. The woman lies down with her arms and chest against the bed or floor and buttocks raised high, and the man penetrates from behind. In addition to ultra-deep penetration that will drive the man crazy, this position allows some of the best stimulation of the woman's G-spot. For a variation, you can lay flat without your buttocks raised, with your man "draping" himself on top of your back. This is a very intimate as well as erotic position for those times when you are in a submissive mood.

The Lotus

The woman sits in her lover's lap, facing him and straddling his erect penis. This position is ideal for extremely deep penetration and passionate kissing. If romantic sex or a feeling of oneness is your aim, the lotus position will make you the lily of his valley.

The Bamboo

The woman lies on her back and places one of her legs on his shoulder, and stretches the other one out straight. Then, she switches her legs and places the other on his shoulder with the other leg stretched out. The continuous alternating of the legs is called "the splitting of the bamboo." You will always see your man's "stalk" growing higher with this one! This is another deep-penetration position and makes for some hot, steamy jungle sex.

The Conch

This is a raised missionary position, great for intimate, eye-to-eye contact. With the woman lying flat on her back, the man sits or kneels between her parted knees. He raises them up and hooks her feet over his thighs.

The Stag

This is a standing position ideal for couples of similar height. This is as hot, intimate, and up close as it gets. Your man catches you, and while he encases you in his arms, he gently forces your knees apart with his as you both sink closely into each other. While leaning against the wall, you may also plant your feet as wide apart as possible, allowing your man easy access for some eager lovemaking. You may wish to gradually shift to sitting in your man's cupped hands, with your arms around his neck and your thighs wrapped around his waist. The direct eye contact, his access to your bottom, and the pressure this position exerts on your clitoris will make your man want to wrap his antler(s) around you.

The Crow

This is a reverse "spooning" position in which the man and woman lie head to toe and side by side, with the man's head at the woman's feet and vice versa. The woman wraps both legs around her man's hips and guides his penis (lingam) into her vagina (yoni). She may rub her breasts against his legs, but lets him control the thrusting movements. This position allows each partner to play with, caress, and otherwise enjoy the other's buttocks. The Crow will make your guy absolutely cuckoo for you.

The Yawning

The man kneels at the edge of the bed in front of the woman while she is on her back. He holds her legs open wide at the ankles and penetrates her from this kneeling position. Highly stimulating for the man, and easy on the woman. Penetration is deep, and the erotic view will definitely not put your man to sleep.

Final Thoughts: Advice From the Sisterhood

21

The voice of experience is a wise voice indeed. Here are a few pearls of wisdom from some older, high-functioning sisters sharing their wisdom and experience. Each was asked: if you could talk to yourself at age 18 or 20, knowing what you know now, what advice would you give yourself regarding men and relationships?

The sexiest quality in a woman, the quality that drives every man of any age wild, is confidence. Real confidence. That certain place within that knows she is the Goddess, who lives and loves and laughs from deep within her being. That's the overflow you want him to see. Guys dig that kind of thing, big time. Always be ready to walk away. I don't mean threats here. Just "be" it, softly and nonverbally. What I'm talking about is a type of Buddhist detachment. When a man can feel that, without you saying it, he will do everything in his power to keep you happy. He loves it because it keeps him "hunting," and in his masculinity. Whether the relationships end or continue, never give away your power, not to men, not to your own insecurities, not to anyone. Start out of the gate in your power.

—Stacie R. Cole, author and SEO
copywriter, Los Angeles, California

I came of age at the beginning of the sexual revolution. My generation tore down walls and worked to abolish stigmas. I believe in balance and only indulging in experiences that you can live with down the road. If I knew at 18 what I know today, I'd have more fun, be prouder of my body, and differentiate between intimacy and those times when I just needed sexual expression.

I would have taken it slower and made sure that the ones I rocked the sheets with would leave me with a positive memory, both mentally and physically.

—Lynda Forbes, author of *The Tarot of Recovery*

Guys are delicate in their own unique way. Don't be judgmental! The best way for a man to learn how to be a great lover is to have a loving, caring and patient woman to teach him. Have fun and enjoy your life. Having a companion is nice, but if you don't know who you are, it isn't a great way to start a solid relationship. Having a relationship that is long lasting and profound starts with knowing Yourself. Get to know who you are first. That's the best relationship you can ever have, really. To Thine Own Self Be True! It's the gift you give to yourself and is passed on to others.

—Julia Cole, radio talk show host

[We should] *take a long, hard look at how traditions and religions can shape a girl's decisions away from what she really wants. There is an implication that to be single too long is a terrible thing* [and] *that a woman is some "appendage" of a man, such as changing your name upon marriage. Things like a hope chest seem*

harmless but it's telling you that you don't deserve to use the "nice stuff" until you land a man. The worst thing, I think, is to start giving up things. I would say NEVER hook up with somebody who has rules for you. And, think carefully about the rules you think are musts for HIM. If I could go back, I would be much truer to myself. So, that means I need to be true to myself NOW and enjoy it!

—Cindy Kelly, singer-songwriter, artist

I loved that time when I was very sexual. Leave your inhibitions at the door and explore. Pleasure is what its all about. For both parties.... Now that I'm 40 I wish it was still like that.

—Dawnice Kern, single mom

A young female should never be in a rush to marry or live with someone until she learns exactly WHO she is and WHAT she wants for her life. It's NOT selfish to take as much time as you need to figure out who you are at the core, and determine what you will—and what you won't—accept in your life. How can you love another completely and honestly if you don't know who YOU are in the deepest recesses of your soul? "If a man loves and cares about you—really loves and cares about

you—he won't try to change who you are and he won't try to change you. True love is when someone loves you for who you are—not for who they want you to be.

—Bev Walton, author of *SunSigns for Writers*

I wish I knew at age 18 that the dreams I had, were actually feasible. That a goal I set could actually come to fruition and blossom into a plan and was close to being in my grasp. My dream was to live and write and paint in N.Y.C., marry Jewish, eat mac and cheese and walk after dinner in Central Park. I'd hear: "You are going need something to 'fall back on.'" I wish I would have had the wisdom to leave my fear behind. I would have listened to my inner voice that was right all along. I would have wondered a lot more, spoken up a little louder, made a bigger deal about the little things in order to make a difference. I would have learned what "Delayed Gratification" meant and integrated it into my life. I would have taken a long walk off that short pier, jumped in the Lake, taken the last cookie and pursued that dream. In two years I will become President of the company my grandfather started over 50 years ago. Life comes full circle and just when you think you lose sight of your dreams, you realize all you

had to do is click your heels together three times...and eat lots of mac and cheese.

—April S. Fried, cosmetic executive

Learn to love yourself first. This helps rid feelings that undermine a successful relationship such as low self esteem and self worth issues. Feelings of neediness and insecurity are such a huge turnoff for men. Self confidence will attract and excite a man much more than dressing sexy. Self confidence allows you to be more selective about the men you choose. In nature, the female always chooses her mate. Not the other way around. Your confidence won't allow you to tolerate or settle for a man that doesn't respect you. You can't fix a man so don't think you're doing him a favor or improving his life and that one day he'll thank you for your noble efforts. If you truly desire a serious relationship, make a man wait until you get to know him more intimately before having sex with him. Not only will he respect you more, you'll challenge him to examine his feelings about whether he wants a relationship with you or if it's just physical attraction. If he won't wait, then he doesn't consider you relationship material and is not worthy of your most valuable possession…YOU!

—Joyce Velez

Remember Turbo Testosterone Tommy from the introduction? That, of course, didn't work out. He droned on for almost two hours during dinner about his ex-girlfriend, and by the end of the evening I knew everything about her allergies, her nicknames, and her preference for soft instead of crunchy Chinese noodles. In addition, he asked that I not call his cell phone because it was still in her name. I eventually did meet my spiritual partner, but not that night. However, that evening was to be a life-changing turning point for me. That evening I realized that there is nothing wrong with being alone. In fact, it can be very nice—ask any Taoist.

Wishing you a lifetime of happiness, luck, and love,

Shelly Wu

Bibliography

Baumeister, R.F. "The enigmatic appeal of sexual masochism: Why people desire pain, bondage, and humiliation in sex." *Journal of Social and Clinical Psychology* 16 (1997): 133–150.

The Complete Kama Sutra. Translation by Alain Danielou. Rochester, Vt.: Park Street Press, 1994.

Chopra, Deepak. *Kama Sutra*. London: Virgin Books Ltd., 2006.

Diagnostic and Statistical Manual of Mental Disorders, Fourth Edition, Text Revision. Washington, D.C.: American Psychiatric Association, 2000.

Frejer, Ernest. *The Edgar Cayce Companion*. New York: Barnes & Noble, Inc., by arrangement with A.R.E. Press, 1995.

Joudry, Patricia, and Maurie D. Pressman, MD. *Twin Souls*. Center City, Minn.: Hazelden, 2000.

Kapleau, Phillip. *Three Pillars of Zen*. New York: John Weatherhill, Inc., 1965.

Masao, Abe. *Zen and Western Thought*. Honolulu, Hawaii: University of Hawaii Press, 1985.

Prophet, Elizabeth Clare. *Soul Mates and Twin Flames*. Corwin Springs, Mont.: Summit University Press, 1999.

Yeshe, Lama, Jonathan Landaw, and Phillip Glass. *Introduction to Tantra: The Transformation of Desire*. Somerville, Mass.: Wisdom Publications, 2001.

Additional Reading

The Alchemist by Paulo Coelho

The Art of Happiness: A Handbook for Living by His Holiness the Dalai Lama and Howard C. Cutler, MD

The Autobiography of a Yogi by Paramahansa Yogananda

Ayurvedic Massage: Traditional Indian Techniques for Balancing Body and Mind by Harish Johari

The Biology of Belief by Bruce Lipton

Care of the Soul by Thomas Moore

Creative Visualization, Living in the Light by Shakti Gawain

The Dancing Wu Li Masters by Gazy Zukav

Demian by Hermann Hesse

Destiny of Souls: New Case Studies of Life Between Lives by Michael Newton

The Divine Blueprint by Robert Perala

The Essential Rumi translated by Coleman Barks

Here and Hereafter by Ruth Montgomery

The Hero Within by Carol Pearson

I Am: The Magic Presence by St. Germain

Initiation by Elizbeth Haich

Lives and Teachings of the Masters of the Far East by Baird Spalding

Love Is Letting Go of Fear by Gerald Jampolsky

Love by Leo Buscaglia

Many Lives, Many Masters by Brian Weiss

The Mind of the Soul Gary Zukav

Only Love Is Real by Brian Weiss

Past Lives/Future Loves by Dick Sutphin

The Power of Myth by Joseph Campbell

The Power of Your Subconscious Mind by Joseph Murphy

Predestined Love by Dick Sutphen

The Prophet by Kahil Gibran

The Re-enchantment of Everyday Life by Thomas Moore

Reunited Across Centuries by Dick Sutphen

The Road Less Traveled by M. Scott Peck, MD

The Seat of the Soul by Gazy Zukav

The Seth Material series by Jane Roberts

Siddhartha by Herman Hesse

Soul Retrieval by Sandra Ingerman

Soul Stories by Gazy Zukav

Spiritual Relationships by Dr. Mark Pitstick

Strangers Among Us by Ruth Montgomery

The Teachings of White Eagle channeled by Grace Cooke

Twin Souls and Soulmates by St. Germain

The Way of the Peaceful Warrior series by Dan Millman

The Way of the Shaman by Michael Harner

What Happens After You Find Your Soulmate? by Susie and Otto Collins

Women Who Run With the Wolves by Clarissa Pinkola-Estes, PhD

A World Beyond by Ruth Montgomery

You can Heal Your Life by Louise Hay

You Were Born Again To Be Together by Dick Sutphin

Your Love Life and Reincarnation by Stephen Petullo

Index

About the Author

Shelly Wu is the author of *Chinese Astrology: Exploring the Eastern Zodiac* and *Chinese Sexual Astrology: Eastern Secrets to Mind-Blowing Sex*, both published by New Page Books. Her columns and feature articles have been distributed by the Associated Press and Wireless Flash News, and have appeared on ABC News and the BBC. She has also been published in *Psychic Interactive*, *Your Stars*, *In Touch*, and *Life*, and can be heard on radio talk shows worldwide. Shelly lives and loves in sunny California.

239